The
Identification
of
1809 William Wright

of
Franklin County, Virginia,
as the
Son of 1792 John Wright
of
Fauquier County, Virginia
and
Elizabeth (Bronaugh)
(Darnall) Wright

Robert N. Grant

HERITAGE BOOKS
2015

HERITAGE BOOKS

AN IMPRINT OF HERITAGE BOOKS, INC.

Books, CDs, and more—Worldwide

For our listing of thousands of titles see our website
at
www.HeritageBooks.com

Published 2015 by
HERITAGE BOOKS, INC.
Publishing Division
5810 Ruatan Street
Berwyn Heights, Md. 20740

International Standard Book Numbers
Paperbound: 978-0-7884-2528-8
Clothbound: 978-0-7884-6146-0

The Identification Of 1809 William Wright Of Franklin County, Virginia, As The Son Of 1792 John Wright Of Fauquier County, Virginia, And Elizabeth (Bronaugh) (Darnall) Wright

by Robert N. Grant

15 Campo Bello Court, Menlo Park, CA 94025

RNGrant@grantandgordon.com

March 23, 2003

This article sets forth the evidence that 1809 William Wright of Franklin County was probably the son of 1792 John Wright of Fauquier County and Elizabeth (Bronaugh) (Darnell) Wright.

There are numerous persons with the surname Wright and similar given names and to keep track of these different people I have adopted the convention of distinguishing Wrights by listing them with their date of death and place of death, the two most commonly available pieces of information. Thus the William Wright who died in 1809 at Franklin County, Virginia, is identified as 1809 William Wright of Franklin County, Virginia. When Virginia was the state of death, Virginia is not listed with the county. That convention is used in this article.

The evidence for the identification of 1809 William Wright of Franklin County as the son of 1792 John Wright of Fauquier County requires a review of a variety of documents from several families and the tracing of various land records in Prince William County and later in Fauquier County. There are ten parts of this analysis:

First, a review of some of the information known about 1792 John Wright of Fauquier County;

Second, the identification of William Wright, the son of 1792 John Wright of Fauquier County, as married to a Mary (_____) Wright;

Third, the identification of Mary (Grant) Wright as the wife of William Wright, the son of 1792 John Wright of Fauquier County;

Fourth, the identification of 1789 William Wright of Spotsylvania County as not the son of 1792 John Wright of Fauquier County;

Fifth, the identification of 1805 William Wright of Fauquier County as not the son of 1792 John Wright of Fauquier County;

Sixth, documentary evidence connecting 1809 William Wright of Franklin County to Fauquier County;

Seventh, similarity of handwriting,

Eighth, suggestive evidence regarding 1809 William Wright of Franklin County and 1845 John Wright of Franklin County and connecting 1845 John Wright of Franklin County to Fauquier County;

Ninth, family naming evidence connecting the Wright and Grant families; and

Tenth, contrary identifications and why they are probably not correct.

In addition, an Eleventh part is included which summarizes in chronological order the information known about 1809 William Wright of Franklin County and Mary (Grant) Wright in northern Virginia.

The further documentation of 1809 William Wright of Franklin County in Bedford County and Franklin County is extensive and is not given in this article, but I will be happy to share that information with other interested researchers and intend to publish that information in the future as part of a work on 1809 William Wright of Franklin County and his descendants.

Part One: Documentation Related To 1792 John Wright Of Fauquier County

1792 John Wright of Fauquier County has been extensively researched and discussed by Charles Arthur Hoppin in three publications:

1) "Some Descendants of Richard Wright, Gentleman, of London, England, and Northumberland, Va., 1655," published in Tyler's Quarterly Historical and Genealogical Magazine, Vol. I, pages 127-141 and 177-191, 1919, and reprinted in Genealogies of Virginia Families From Tyler's Quarterly Historical and Genealogical Magazine, published by Genealogical Publishing Company, Baltimore, Maryland, 1981;

2) "The Washington-Wright Connection and Some Descendants of Maj. Francis and Anne (Washington) Wright," published in Tyler's Quarterly Historical and Genealogical Magazine, Vol. IV, pages 315-356, 1923, and reprinted in Genealogies of

<u>Virginia Families From Tyler's Quarterly Historical and Genealogical Magazine</u>, published by Genealogical Publishing Company, Baltimore, Maryland, 1981; and

        3)   <u>The Washington Ancestry and Records of The McClain, Johnson, and Forty Other Colonial American Families</u>, prepared for Edward Lee McClain, and printed by Yale University Press, 1932.

        However, Charles Hoppin's materials should be read carefully and with caution. He made a number of mistaken identifications, some of which will be discussed below, and sometimes extrapolated conclusions beyond what the evidence supported.

        1792 John Wright of Fauquier County has also been discussed by Ann Reed Ritchie in her work <u>Major Francis Wright And Ann Washington With Allied Families</u>, 1973.

        1792 John Wright of Fauquier County has also been discussed by Myrtle Viola (Sears) Steiner and Velma (Wright) Ellis Wakefield in their work <u>Wright-Washington and Allied Families "Descendants of Capt. Richard Wright - From the Eastern Shore of Virginia to the Pacific Coast of California 1630-1967"</u>, undated but apparently published in 1967.

        The following information on 1792 John Wright of Fauquier County does not discuss all of the information available about this person, but only those portions relevant to identifying his son William Wright.

        A.   **His Parents 1729/30 John Wright Of Stafford County And Dorothy (_____) Wright**

        1792 John Wright of Fauquier County was probably the son of 1729/30 John Wright of Stafford County and Dorothy (____) Wright.

        The three works by Charles Arthur Hoppin contain an extensive discussion of 1729/30 John Wright of Stafford County and the extant documentation relating to his life. Only the documentation relevant to this discussion is reviewed here.

        On August 27, 1723, at Westmoreland County, Virginia, D.& W.B. 7/292, 1729/30 John Wright of Stafford County exchanged his 800 acres of land in Cople Parish, Westmoreland County, for 1000 acres of land owned by Henry Lee on Powell's Run in Stafford County:

"This Indenture made the twenty seventh day of August in the year of Our Lord One thousand seven hundred and twenty three . . . . Between John Wright of the County of Westmorld in Virginia gentleman of the One part and Henry Lee of the County of Westmorld aforesaid gentleman of the Other part Witnesseth that the said John Wright for and in consideracon of the Exchange for One thousand acres of land in Stafford County scituate lying and being on Powells run whereon the said Henry Lee hath now a plantacon or quarter as also for the Consideration of two hundred pounds sterl: money of great Britain ten thousand pounds of Tobacco and five negro or mulatto slaves . . . . have granted . . . . unto the said Henry Lee . . . . One peice parcell tract or dividend of land scituate lying and being in Cople parish in the aforesaid County of Westmorld and on the mouth of lower machitique river containing by estimacon eight hundred acres be the same more or less being part of a pattent of land formerly granted to Mr. John Mottrom by pattent bearing date the thirteenth day of August in the year of Our Lord sixteen hundred and fifty and since by several mean Conveyances or decents become the proper right and inheritance of the said John Wright and is the plantacon and tract of land whereon he now lives excepting one half acre of the said land being the grave yard on the manour plantacon where Majr Francis Wright father of the said John is buryed as also One other part of the said dividend of land Known by the name of time Neck which the said John Wright hath allready given to his brother Richard Wright by deeds bearing date the twenty second day of September in the year of our Lord seventeen hundred and fourteen which said deeds are recorded in the County Court records of Westmorland which may fully appear recourse being thereunto had. . . .

Westmorld County SS

At a Court held for the said County the 28th day of August 1723 - John Wright gentleman personally acknowledged the exchange and sale of Land from him to Henry Lee gentleman to be his proper act and deed together with the livery and seizen and receipt of Consideracon money thereon endorsed. And Thomas Sorrell by virtue of a power of attorney proved by the Wittnesses relinquished the dower and thirds at the Comon Law of Dorothy wife of the said John in and to the lands and prmisses by the said deed conveyed all which at the instance of the said Lee is admitt to record . . . ."

This record identifies John Wright's father as Francis Wright, his wife as Dorothy (_____) Wright, and his residence before 1723 as on the mouth of the Lower Machodoc River in Cople Parish of Westmoreland County.

The death of John Wright in 1729 or 1730 at Stafford County, Virginia, is evidenced by the following discussion from The Washington Ancestry at page 386:

4

". . . ."Liber K. 1721 to 1730" and "Liber L. 1728 to 1731" - the original books of the recording of wills administrationships, appraisals, inventories, settlements, and distributions of the estates of testates and intestates, and of orders of court, etc., of the county of Stafford are among the record books of that county between 1709 and 1744 long since lost. The alphabetical index to the documents recorded in Liber K is still extant down to a portion of the entries under the letter W. The index to Liber L is preserved except for the letters A and B. The extant index to both libers is entitled, "General Index, 1721-45," and the indexes to libers K and L follow one another. The index to Liber K indicates that the lost book comprised a little over 300 pages of records. Near the end of the lost Liber K, 1721 to 1730, at its page 269, was recorded, as the extant index to that liber bears witness, "John Wright's Inventory, 269." The position of page 269 in the lost book shows that the inventory was taken, presented in court, accepted, and ordered recorded in 1729 or 1730. This evidence is proof of the death, in 1729 or 1730, of John[3] Wright, Senior, of the Leesylvania plantation on Powell's Run. The plantation then and until July 9, 1730, was located in Stafford County, and on that day and afterward in Prince William County. Directly beneath the index entry referring to the inventory as having been recorded at page 269 of the lost Liber K, is another entry, viz., "Wright's A/C vs Wright's Estate - 285." This record refers to the administrator's acount of the administration of the estate of John[3] Wright. . . ."

This seems to be adequate evidence to establish that John Wright died in 1729 or 1730 in Stafford County.

On July 9, 1730, the Virginia Assembly authorized the creation from Stafford County of Hamilton Parish, to be effective January 1, 1730/31, and Prince William County, to be effective March 25, 1731. The land of 1729/30 John Wright of Stafford County on Powell's Run was located within that new parish and new county.

Charles Hoppin in The Washington Ancestry further stated that on April 27, 1731, a John Wright was nominated as a justice of the new county of Prince William:

"The following record of the action of the Governor and Council is taken from *Virginia Council Orders*, V, 1420-1447, 1448:

1731, April 27. The Governor, with the advice of the Council is pleas'd to nominate Justices of the peace for the new erected County of Prince William, viz: Thomas Harrison, Dennis McCarty, Willm Linton, Francis Awbry, Robert Jones, Burr Harrison, & Moses Quarles of the Quorum; and Leonard Barker, Wm Harrison, Valentine Barker, John Wright, John Allen, Willm Hackney, and Joseph Hudnal. Gent."

Since 1729/30 John Wright had died prior to this appointment of justices of the peace for Prince William County, the John Wright of this appointment was not 1729/30 John Wright. Charles Hoppin concluded that the appointment was of John Wright, the son of 1729/30 John Wright of Stafford County. That son John would have been residing on the land acquired by his father 1729/30 John Wright in the new county and the appointment would have been in honor of the father, who had been a justice of Westmoreland County as had 1729/30 John Wright's father 1713 Francis Wright of Westmoreland County.

Charles Hoppin supported that identification with a references in two deeds from 1742 Francis Wright of Prince William County. Under the law of primogeniture, the land of an intestate passed to the eldest son. Two deeds for the sale of the land originally purchased by 1729/30 John Wright of Stafford County by Westmoreland Deed 7/192 make clear that 1729/30 John Wright of Stafford County died intestate and that Francis Wright inherited that land as the eldest son of 1729/30 John Wright of Stafford County.

On May 28, 1739, at Prince William County, Virginia, D.B. D/129 Francis Wright and his wife Anne sold 333 acres of the 1000 acres of land purchased by his father John Wright from Henry Lee:

> "This Indenture made the twenty eighth day of May in the year of our Lord one thousand seven hundred & thirty nine Between Francis Wright of the parish of Hamilton in the County of Prince William planter & Anne his wife of the one part and Benjamin Grayson of the parish & County aforesaid Gent. of the other part Witnesseth that the said Francis Wright & Anne his wife for & in Consideration of the sum of one hundred pounds Sterling . . . . doth Grant . . . . unto the said Benjamin Grayson . . . . all that plantation tract or parcel of land containing three hundred & thirty three acres situate lying & being on Powels Creek in the County of Prince William aforesaid, it being the third part of one thousand acres of land formerly sold & conveyed by Henry Lee unto John Wright deced. father to the afsd. Francis Wright party to these presents as by Deed dated the twenty fifth day of June MDCCXXV doth & may more fully & at large appear . . . ."

This deed clearly identifies the land involved as the same as that purchased by 1729/30 John Wright of Stafford County in 1723 and identifies Francis Wright as his son.

On July 27, 1741, at Prince William County, Virginia, D.B. E/339 Francis Wright sold the remaining 667 acres of land back to Henry Lee:

"This Indenture made the twenty Seventh day of July . . . . One thousand Seven hundred & forty one Between Francis Wright of Hamilton parish in Prince William County planter of the one part & Henry Lee of Cople parish in Westmorland County Gent of the other part Witnesseth that for & in Consideration of the Sum of Two hundred and Sixty pounds . . . . doth give grant enfeof & Confirm unto the said Henry Lee . . . . all that . . . . Land . . . . containing Six hundred Sixty Seven acres Scituate lying & being in the aforesaid parish of Hamilton & County of Prince William & is bounded or incuded between two Creeks now known & Called by the names of powels Creek & Nyapscoe Creek also binding on a parcel of Land the said Francis Wright sold to Mr. Benjamin Gresham the said Six hundred and Sixty Seven acres of Land being part of One thousand acres of Land Conveyed by the abovesaid Henry Lee to John Wright (father of the aforesaid Francis) in fee Simple as by Deed dated the twelfth day of June annog Domini One thousand Seven hundred & twenty five relation being thereunto _____ more fully & at Large appear & the said John Wright father of the said Francis Wright dying intestate the said Francis Wright as his eldest Son is heir at Law to the said Land . . . ."

Charles Hoppin noted that the reference in the deed to "the said John Wright father of the said Francis Wright dying intestate the said Francis Wright as his eldest Son is heir at Law to the said Land" suggested that Francis Wright was not the only son, but the eldest son and, therefore, there existed another son. If there had been no other son, then the deed probably would have recited that Francis Wright was John Wright's only son. The most probable person for that other son of 1729/30 John Wright of Stafford County would have been the John Wright appointed as a justice of the peace for the county in 1731.

While the evidence is not as strong as one would like, it seems fair to conclude that John Wright was a son of 1729/30 John Wright of Stafford County.

On March 23, 1740, at Prince William County, Virginia, D.B. E/170 John Wright purchased 236 acres of land in Hamilton Parish from Jeremiah Darnall and his wife Catharine:

"This Indenture made this 23d day of March . . . . one thousand seven hundred & forty Between Jeremiah Darnal of ye parish of Hamilton & County of Prince William planter & Catharine his wife of the one part and John Wright of the aforementioned parish & County Gent. of the other part Witnesseth that the said

Jeremiah Darnal & Catharine his wife . . . . sell . . . . unto the said John Wright . .
. . all that tract or parcel of land containing two hundred & thirty six acres situate
lying & being ye parish of Hamilton & County of Prince William being part of a
greater tract taken up by Waugh Darnall father to ye said Jeremiah and is
bounded as followeth Vizt. Beginning at a Red Oak standing in Colonel Corbins
line . . . ."

As will be set forth below, the deposition of 1792 John Wright of Fauquier County made
in 1790 identifies this land as his. Charles Hoppin asserted that the purchase of this
236 acres of land shortly before the sale by Francis Wright of the remainder of 1000
acres of land that had belonged to 1729/30 John Wright of Stafford County indicated
the establishment by John Wright of his own residence following the death of 1729/30
John Wright's widow Dorothy. No other land purchases by a John Wright in Prince
William County existed before this 1740 deed and since the John Wright appointed as a
justice of the peace in 1731 would have most likely resided in Prince William County,
the only place he could have lived would have been on the land of 1729/30 John Wright
of Stafford County. The conclusion that 1792 John Wright of Fauquier County was the
same person as John Wright, the son of 1729/30 John Wright of Stafford County, thus
appears reasonable.

However, there is in the Stafford County Index for Will and Deed Book L at page
492 a deed from Grant to Wright dated 1728 to 1731. This may have been for land
which later became part of Prince William County and may have been a deed to
1729/30 John Wright of Stafford County or it may have been a deed to a different John
Wright who happened to be the John Wright appointed as a justice of the new Prince
William County in 1731. And the deed may have been to someone named Wright, but
not John Wright. No disposition of this land is listed in the Stafford County Deed Index.
There are sufficient gaps in the Prince William County deeds that the given name of a
person named Wright who might have disposed of this land cannot be determined.

The result of this discussion is to leave the identification of 1792 John Wright of
Fauquier County as the son of 1729/30 John Wright of Stafford County as probable, but
not as certain as Charles Hoppin asserted in his works.

The Washington Ancestry by Charles Arthur Hoppin stated at page 394 that the mother of 1792 John Wright of Fauquier County was Dorothy (Awbrey) Wright:

> "John[4] Wright (John[3], Francis[2], Richard[1]), vestryman, captain, justice, and sheriff, was born in the "great house" on the Wright "manour plantation" on the Lower Machodoc peninsula in Westmoreland County as has been indicated, *circa* 1707, his parents, John[3] and Dorothy (Awbrey) Wright, having married about the year 1705, and his brother Francis[4] having been born as their eldest son, there being no evidence as to there being daughters by this marriage."

This statement is partially incorrect. Westmoreland County Deed 7/292 establishes only that 1729/30 John Wright's wife was a Dorothy Wright, not necessarily Dorothy (Awbrey) Wright. Charles Hoppin in The Washington Ancestry identified Dorothy Awbrey as the wife of 1729/30 John Wright of Stafford County by a process of elimination and not by documented evidence:

> "One event was the second marriage of Francis[2] to Martha Cox, and the other the marriage (about 1705) of John[3] to a Dorothy, probably Dorothy Awbrey.*
>
> *This marriage occurred about 1705. The exact date is not recorded as the records of marriage licenses, and bonds, and of the parish churches for Westmoreland are lost. Other records indicate the fact of the marriage. It has required exhaustive search and study to determine the identity of John[3] Wright's wife Dorothy, because of the prevalence in the Northern Neck of Virginia of women named Dorothy. Seventeen Dorothys of marriageable age, *circa* 1705, appear in the records. The surnames of these Dorothys were Ransone, Gouldman, Armstrong, Henry, Ripley, Dudley, Gatewood, Smith, Baughan, Durham, Strother, Maclanan, Abbott, and Awbrey. No one of these Dorothys, save the last, extant records show, could be the Dorothy who married John[3] Wright. The last one, Dorothy Awbrey, by a process of exclusion is decided to be the wife of John[3] Wright.
>
> Dorothy[3] Awbrey was a granddaughter of Henry[1] Awbrey (sometimes written Aubrey, Awbury, Aubery, and Awberry - Aubry and Aubrey being the spelling in Virginia of the name of another Aubry family that came direct from France). . . . Our particular interest is in the son, Richard[2] Awbrey, as he was the father of Dorothy[3] Awbrey who, it is believed, married about 1705 John[3] Wright. . . ."

A deed from Essex County establishes that this identification of Dorothy Awbrey as the wife of 1729/30 John Wright of Stafford County and the daughter of Richard Awbrey and granddaughter of Henry Awbrey was incorrect. Essex County, Virginia, Deed 19/28 dated February 11, 1729, provided as follows:

"To all Christian people to whom this present Indenture shall come Know ye that John Billups & Dorithy my wife of the parish of St. Ann's in the County of Essex within the Colony of Virginia Daughter & heir Apparant of Richd. Aubery Decd Son of Henry Aubery Decd. . . . .

Signed Sealed &	)	Jno. Billop		
Delivered In the	)		her	
In the presence	)	Dorithy	X	Billips
of us	)			
Joseph Lovill				
Edward White				
Mark Morgan				

At a Court held for Essex County on the 17th Day of June 1729 John Billups and Dorithy his wife Acknowledged this their Indented release of Land to James Garnett Gentl. which on his Motion is Admitted to record

Test
W Beverley C Cur"

This record clearly identifies Dorothy Awbrey, the daughter of Richard Awbrey and granddaughter of Henry Awbrey, as the wife of John Billups in 1729 and necessarily not the wife of 1729/30 John Wright of Stafford County.

Wright-Washington and Allied Families by Myrtle Steiner and Velma Wakefield at pages 28 and 29 stated that Captain John (3) Wright, meaning 1792 John Wright of Fauquier County, married Dorothy Awbrey and she was the daughter of Francis Awbrey and granddaughter of Thomas Awbrey:

"Capt. John (3) Wright
. . . .
John Wright married between 1705/6 Dorothy Awbrey.
. . . .
Dorothy Awbrey was a daughter of Francis Awbrey, Prince William County, son of Thomas and Jemimia Awbrey, who was the son of Peter and Alice Awbrey, England and America."

No documentation or source was cited for these statements and it is unclear what the authors relied on for this identification.

The result is that the maiden name of 1792 John Wright's mother Dorothy (_____) Wright remains unknown.

B. **His Birth**

1792 John Wright of Fauquier County was born before October 2, 1700, or in about 1700.

On October 2, 1790, in the case of Darnall v. Turberville, Prince William County, Virginia, Land Causes 1789-93/358, John Wright gave his deposition in connection with a survey of the lands in dispute between the parties:

". . . .

Fauquier Sct

The Deposition of Capt John Wright aged ninety years and upwards Deposed and sayeth that a red oak that he is now at that he the said Deponent has heard it called Colo. Corbins line for sixty years and upwards and he bought land of Jeremiah Darnall by this said line at Colo. Corbins and further saith not

John Wright

Fauquier Sct.

This day Capt. John Wright made oath in presence of Jeremiah Darnall Pltf and George Turberville Deft to the above given under my hand this 2d day of October 1790

Jo Blackwell

Fauquier Sct.

The Deposition of Capt. John Wright aged ninety years and upward Deposed and sayeth that the old field he now shows has been cleared about forty five years ago by Colo. Corbins Overseers and this Deponent further saith not

John Wright

Fauquier Sct.

This day Capt. John Wright made oath in presence of Jeremiah Darnall Pltf and George Tuberville Deft given under my hand this 2d day October 1790.

Jo Blackwell"

This deposition was also published in <u>Prince William County Land Causes 1789-1793</u> by Sam Sparacio.

As set forth above, on March 23, 1740, at Prince William County, Virginia, D.B. E/170 1792 John Wright of Fauquier County purchased 236 acres of land from Jeremiah and Catharine Darnall. The references in the deposition to the land John Wright purchased of Jeremiah Darnall and to the land being adjacent to Colonel Corbin's land identify the John Wright of these depositions as 1792 John Wright of Fauquier County. The result is that these depositions establish that 1792 John Wright of Fauquier County was born before October 2, 1700.

However, John A. Washington correctly noted that the reference to John Wright being "aged ninety years and upwards" was an introductory statement by Joseph Blackwell and not part of the deposition of John Wright. The age stated may have been an estimate of Joseph Blackwell rather than a statement by the deponent himself. In addition, John A. Washington and Dr. Luke F. Wright both stated that it is not unusual when persons become older to tend to exagerrate their age, feeling "a secret delight in surviving our contemporaries and even our juniors." Both points are well taken and in recognition of that, the date of birth must also be given as circa 1700.

<u>The Washington Ancestry</u> by Charles Arthur Hoppin stated at page 394 that 1792 John Wright of Fauquier County was born in about 1707 as the son of 1729/30 John Wright of Stafford County and Dorothy (Awbrey) Wright:

> "John[4] Wright (John[3], Francis[2], Richard[1]), vestryman, captain, justice, and sheriff, was born in the "great house" on the Wright "manour plantation" on the Lower Machodoc peninsula in Westmoreland County as has been indicated, *circa* 1707, his parents, John[3] and Dorothy (Awbrey) Wright, having married about the year 1705, and his brother Francis[4] having been born as their eldest son, there being no evidence as to there being daughters by this marriage."

This statement is incorrect in two respects.

As set forth above, 1792 John Wright of Fauquier County by his own deposition stated that he was born before October 2, 1700. Charles Hoppin's listing of the date of birth in about 1707 was simply an extrapolation of an estimated date of birth based on the estimated marriage date of an incorrectly identified marriage. <u>The Washington</u>

12

Ancestry at pages 366 and 370 also stated that 1729/30 John Wright of Stafford County's sons Francis and John were born between 1705 and 1708:

> "Of the marriages of Francis Wright and his son John, which marriage occurred first can not be definitely determined. Doubtless the marriage of John occurred first. That the two events were not more than two years apart is evident from the fact that Francis[4] Wright and John[4] Wright, the two sons of John[3] Wright, are shown by records to have been born between 1705 and 1708; . . . ."

It is unclear what records Charles Hoppin was relying on that showed the dates of birth of the sons Francis Wright and John Wright as between 1705 and 1708. A review of the remainder of The Washington Ancestry disclosed no such records to support those asserted dates of birth. The John Wright deposition in 1790 suggests that there were no such records and that Charles Hoppin made assertions that were not supported by the evidence.

This last conclusion is bolstered by a prior work of Charles Hoppin. The Washington Ancestry was published in 1932 and incorporated material from the two articles in Tyler's Quarterly cited above. In "Some Descendants of Richard Wright, Gentleman, of London, England, and Northumberland, Va., 1655," published in 1919 Charles Hoppin asserted that 1792 John Wright was born in about 1712:

> "John[4] Wright (John 3, Francis 2, Richard 1), "Gent.," "Churchwarden," "Captain," "Sheriff" and "Justice" of Prince William county, and later "Justice" of Fauquier county, was born in Cople parish, Westmoreland county, Virginia, about 1712, his father having married his mother Dorothy between 1707 and 1710."

This 1712 birth date is inconsistent with Mr. Hoppin's later conclusion in The Washington Ancestry that the birth date was about 1707 and once again, no documentation was given for this birth date.

C.   **His Wife Elizabeth (Bronaugh) (Darnall) Wright, Widow Of Waugh Darnell**

1792 John Wright of Fauquier County married Elizabeth (Bronaugh) Darnell, the daughter of Jeremiah Bronaugh and the widow of Waugh Darnell, sometime after October 7, 1726, and before April 14, 1736. The evidence for this was first set forth in <u>The Darnall, Darnell Family</u> compiled by Avlyn Dodd Conley and requires the review of several different documents.

The will of Waugh Darnell was dated on June 2, 1726, probated on October 7, 1726, at King George County, Virginia, Ct.O.B. 1/333, and provided as follows:

"This Last Will & Testament of Waugh Darnall is; I leave to my Son Jeremiah Darnall the Tract of Land on Where I live That a Tract of Land Lying on Deadera Run may be divided Between my daughters Anne Darnall Margaret Darnall & their heirs for Ever I Likewise desire that my five Negros with their Issue may Equally be divided Between my Wife & my Children I Likewise desire that my father & Mother May have ye(?) Equal Mentanance with my Wife & Likewise if my wife Should dey That my father & Mother Should have an Equal Mantanance with my Children under the Disposal of Thomas Stone Likewise I Desire that my father & mother With my Wife & Children may Live on this plantation Likewise I Desire that if the Lord be Pleased to call my Wife to him yt Thomas Stone may be Sole Executor Over my Children Likewise I Desire yt. all my Goods & Chattells may Equally Divided between my Wife & my Children this is my Last Will & Testament this Second Day of June in the Year of Our Lord God One Thousand Seven hundred & twenty Six as Witness my hand & Seale Likewise I Desire if Thomas Stone Should Dey yt my Children Should be Brought under the family of Bronaugh

Witnesses present   Waugh Darnall
Charles Traners
          his
Thimothy   Sulivan
          Mark

At a Court held for King George County on Friday ye 7th Day of Octr Anno Dom 1726

The last Will & Testament of Waugh Darnall Deced was presented into Court by Elizabeth his widow & Executrix who made Oath thereto & the same was proved by the Oaths of Charles Traners & Thomas Stone & Admitted to Record

          Copy Test
          T. Turner Cl Cur"

This record identifies Elizabeth (_____) Darnell as the widow of Waugh Darnall and identifies Jeremiah Darnall, Ann Darnall, and Margaret Darnall as his children.

The will of Jeremiah Bronaugh was dated on April 14, 1736, probated on January 5, 1749, at King George County, Virginia, W.B. A-1/228, and provided as follows:

> "In the Name of God Amen I Jeremiah Bronaugh of the County of King George in the Parish of Brunswick . . . .
>
> Item To my Daughter Elizabeth Wright I Give four ew's & no more because she has had her full share of my Estate already
>
> . . . .
>
> At a Court held for King George County on Friday January 5, 1749
>
> The Last Will and Testament of Jeremiah Bronnaugh deceased was presented into Court by David Bronaugh his Executor who made Oath thereto and the same was proved by the Oaths of John Champe Gent. and Anderson Doniphan and Admitted to Record
>
> > Copa Test
> > Harry Turner Cl Cur"

This record identifies Jeremiah Bronaugh's daughter Elizabeth Bronaugh as married to _____ Wright by April 14, 1736.

The identification of Elizabeth (Bronaugh) (Darnell) Wright as the wife of 1792 John Wright was confirmed by the case of Smith vs. Darnall's Executors, Fauquier County, Virginia, Chancery Court, Papers terminating February 1802, which The Darnall, Darnell Family stated included the following Bill in Chancery by Augustine Smith:

> "Augustine Smith of Fauquier County sayeth in 1781 he served in the Virginia Militia and became entitled for his said service to a certificate -8:10:0, and being anxious to become an adventurer in Kentucky lands mentioned same to Jeremiah Darnall, now deceased, and he said Jeremiah Darnall proposed to assist him in locating the said land thru Major James Wright who was then about to go to Kentucky for the purpose of locating lands, ... but being so nearly connected with the said Jeremiah as to have married his daughter and being also connected by marriage to the said James Wright . . . ."

As will be set forth below, James Wright was a son of 1792 John Wright of Fauquier County and thus Augustine Smith was connected by marriage to 1792 John Wright of Fauquier County.

On May 22, 1797, at Fauquier County, Virginia, Chancery Court Loose Papers, File Folder 1/15, James Wright filed his answer to the complaint in Smith v. Darnall as follows:

"The Answer of James Wright Exr of Jeremiah Darnall to the bill of Complt by Augustine Smith Complt . . . . This Defendnt knows it to be true that the sd Jeremiah Died possessed of the Quantity of Kentucky land stated in the Complts bill and he believes it to be the whole he did own This Defendt recollects that in the year 1783 when he made known his Intention of visiting Kentuckey for the purpose of locating & surveying lands that the sd Jeremiah applied to him to know if he procured a warrant whether this Defendt would locate & survey it and that on this Defendts giving his assent he shortly after procured a warrant for the amount stated in the Complts bill This Defendt located the same & surveyed the lands without making any charge for his services or trouble, demaning no more than his expences & costs which was paid by said Jeremiah. Had this Defendt known that the land was for the Complt, he does not think he should have done the business on the same terms The sd Jeremiah was a half brother of this Defendt & therefore he was induced to ask of him no more than his expences . . . .

The within answer was sworn to before me by James Wright this 22d May 1797

Fauquier Sc.

James Wright Executor of Jeremiah Darnall made oath before me that the within Answer Contains the whole truth and nothing but the truth to the best of his knowledge. Given under my hand this 22d May 1797.

Wm. Edmonds Jr."

For James Wright, the son of 1792 John Wright of Fauquier County and Elizabeth Wright, to have been the half-brother of Jeremiah Darnall, the son of Waugh Darnell and his wife Elizabeth Darnell, James Wright's mother Elizabeth would have had to have been the wife of both Waugh Darnell and 1792 John Wright. With the listing in Jeremiah Bronaugh's will of his daughter as Elizabeth Wright, the identification would seem complete that 1792 John Wright's wife was Elizabeth (Bronaugh) (Darnall) Wright.

The Washington Ancestry stated at page 401 that 1792 John Wright of Fauquier County married Elizabeth Darnall and that she was a daughter of Waugh Darnall:

"He [referring to John[4] Wright] may have bought the Darnall land because he had married Elizabeth Darnall. There is no record proof of this marriage; as none is likely to be discovered, we need not go beyond the expression of the belief that the Elizabeth named in the will of Captain John[4] Wright as his wife was a daughter of Waugh Darnall,* and sister of the Jeremiah Darnall, who sold Captain Wright a share of the estate of the deceased Waugh Darnall, thus still closer drawing these families together."

As is apparent, Charles Hoppin offered no evidence for his identification of Elizabeth Waugh as a daughter of Waugh Darnall, rather than his widow, and the identification as such was mere speculation on Charles Hoppin's part and, based on the evidence set forth above, incorrect.

D.   **His Land Transactions**

As set forth above, on March 23, 1740, at Prince William County, Virginia, D.B. E/170 John Wright purchased 236 acres of land from Jeremiah Darnall, the son of Waugh Darnall, and Jeremiah's wife Catharine Darnall:

"This Indenture made this 23d day of March in the fourteenth year . . . . one thousand seven hundred & forty Between Jeremiah Darnal of ye parish of Hamilton & County of Prince William planter & Catharine his wife of the one part and John Wright of the aforementioned parish & County Gent. of the other part Witnesseth that the said Jeremiah Darnal & Catharine his wife for and in consideration of the sum of sixty pounds . . . . sell . . . . unto the said John Wright . . . . all that tract or parcel of land containing two hundred & thirty six acres situate lying & being ye parish of Hamilton & County of Prince William being part of a greater tract taken up by Waugh Darnall father to ye said Jeremiah and is bounded as followeth Vizt. Beginning at a Red Oak standing in Colonel Corbins line . . . ."

The Washington Ancestry by Charles Arthur Hoppin also referred to this land purchase:

"Twenty-one months after Francis[4] Wright had sold one-third of the Wright estate, his brother John[4] Wright, doubtless aware that Francis was negotiating to sell the remaining two-thirds, purchased a home for himself four months before Francis sold the said two-thirds to Henry Lee. In the record of this deed it will be noted that John[4] Wright is described as "Captain" and "Gentleman." This title "Captain," means that he was a justice of the county of Prince William, as the justices had authority in and over the county militia with the rank of "Captain" and "Major" according to whether or not they were of the quorum among the justices. The use of this title in 1740 implies that John[4] Wright was still a justice after his first appointment in 1731.

17

[Prince William County, Deed Book E, p. 170. Abstract]:

[Endorsed]: Darnall To Wright, Release 7th Decr. 1745. Dd to Capt. Wright

Indenture made 23 March . . . . 1740 . . . whereby Jeremiah Darnall of ye Parish of Hamilton & County of Prince William, Planter, & Catherine his wife, . . . sell . . . . . to John Wright of the aforementioned Parish & County, Gent. . . . 236 acres scituate in ye Parish of Hamilton & County of Prince William being part of a greater tract taken up by Waugh Darnall, father to ye said Jeremiah . . . Vizt. Beginning at a Red Oak standing in Colonel Corbins line, & extending thence along the said line South 88 degrees West 414 poles to a Hicory & Gum in ye said Corbin's line . . . .

Jeremiah Darnall

. . . .

Acknowledged in open court March 23d 1740.

This tract of land to which John[4] Wright removed in 1741, from the estate of his deceased father three miles north of Dumfries, is situated about twenty miles west of Dumfries, and about twenty-eight miles south of the Bull Run estate of his brother, Francis[4] Wright. The fact that Captain Wright was a vestryman, a county officer, and a justice, and so continued for thirty years, in addition to being a gentleman farmer, suggests that in removing farther away from the first county courthouse at the ferry on the Occoquan, on the Mason land later known as Woodbridge, he must have had supreme reasons. The first reason was that his brother had sold out the land from under their feet and the roof from over their heads. He may have bought the Darnall land because he had married Elizabeth Darnall. There is no record proof of this marriage; as none is likely to be discovered, we need not go beyond the expression of the belief that the Elizabeth named in the will of Captain John[4] Wright as his wife was a daughter of Waugh Darnall,* and sister of the Jeremiah Darnall, who sold Captain Wright a share of the estate of the deceased Waugh Darnall, thus still closer drawing these families together. . . ."

On July 22, 1748, at Prince William County, Virginia, D.B. L/44 and L/46 John Wright received a conveyance of 60 acres of land from Charles Garner and Ann (Darnall) (Williams) Garner, land which was part of a patent deed previously granted to Waugh Darnall and adjoining land which John Wright had previously purchased from Jonas Williams, Jr., and his wife Anne (Darnall) Williams:

"This Indenture made the 22d day of July . . . . one thousand seven hundred & forty eight Between Charles Garner & Anne his wife of the County of Prince

William & Colony of Virginia of the one part & John Wright gent. of the County & Colony aforesd. of the other part Witnesseth that the said Charles Garner & Anne his wife . . . . doth grant . . . . unto the sd. John Wright one peice or parcel of Land Containing Sixty Acres Scituate lying & being in Prince William County aforeaid being part of a tract of Land by patent from the proprietors office granted to Waugh Darnal deced & Joyning to the sd. John Wrights land wh he formerly purchased of Jonas Williams Junr & the sd. Anne relation being had to the records of the aforesaid County of Prince William will more fully appear . . . ."

On August 26, 1751, at Prince William County, Virginia, D.B. M/169 John Wright gave 185 acres of land to his son William Wright, land which included the 60 acres of Prince William Deeds L/44 and L/46:

". . . . Know ye that . . . . for and in consideration of the natural love and affection which I have and Do bear unto my dear beloved son William Wright . . . . grant and confirm unto the sd. William Wright all that messuage tract or parcel of Land which he now lives on containing one hundred and Eighty five acres Situate lying and being in the parish of hamilton and county of Prince William and Collony of Virginia and Bounded as followeth Beginning at two red oaks being the dividing corner between Jonas Williams and Scimon Morgan and runs with the dividing line S: 7-1/2 degrees W: 185 poles to a box oak on a branch thence N. 83 d:w: 208 poles to a Chesnut on a hill in the old Line of the deeds thence with the line of the deeds to the beginning it being part of a greater Dividant taken up by Waugh Darnal, Decd. by patent Dated the 17th day of febewary 1725 . . . . in Witness whereof I hereunto set my hand & fixed my seal this 26th day of August AD 1751

John Wright

Test. John Crump Weeden Smith

At a Court held for the County of Prince William 26° august 1751 John Wright Gent acknowledged this Deed which is admitted to record

Test

Z. Wagener Cl

Deed dld. Mr. Wm Wright & wife ye 20th May 1762."

The execution of the deed in 1751 and the delivery to William Wright in 1762 indicate that William Wright was present in Hamilton Parish at both times and the description in the deed of William Wright as living on the land at the time the deed was executed indicates that he was old enough in 1751 to be occupying his own farm.

E.   His Death And Will

The will of John Wright was dated on June 1, 1785, probated on February 27, 1792, at Fauquier County, Virginia, W.B. 2/219, and provided as follows:

> ". . . . I John Wright of the Parish of Hamilton & County of Fauquier . . . . do make this my last will . . . . I give and desire and bequeath to my son James Wright all of that my land lying on the east side of the run, being part of the tract of land whereon I now live, in the County of Fauquier to him his Heirs & assigns forever. I also give to my son James Wright one negroe named tom and one negro named Moses to him his Heirs or assigns for ever,
>
> Item I give to my grand daughter Betsey Wright daughter to my son James Wright one negro named Jinny to her, her Heirs and assigns forever.
>
> Item I give likewise to my two daughters Mary Wright & Rosamond Wright the plantation whereon I now live and all the land I hold lying on the west side of the said run above mentioned to them & their Heirs lawfully begotten of their bodys forever to be divided between the two as they can agree, and in case they die without such Heir. It is my Will and desire that the said land shall go to my son James Wright to him his Heirs & assigns for ever.
>
> Item I give to my two daughters Mary Wright & Rosamond Wright the negroes as followeth, Vz. Dinah, Jude Ledie, Robin, Lucy, Will & Milley to them their Heirs and assigns forever, and all Future increes of the aforesaid negroes to the aforesaid Mary and Rosamond Wright their heirs and assigns forever to be divided by the two as they can agree.
>
> I likewise give to my aforesaid two Daughters Mary Wright & Rosamond Wright all my house hold Furniture such as beds &c and all my stock such as horses cattle, sheep & Hogues to them their Heirs and assigns for ever.
>
> Item I give to my son William Wright and my son John Wright twenty shillings each current money of Virginia the reason why I have left my two sons William and John Wright no more is that I gave them both land which they sold.
>
> Item it is my will and desire that in case my daughter Elizabeth Parlow should ever apply that then my executors pay her fifteen pounds out of my estate, current money of Virginia. It is my will & desire that all my estate heretofore mentioned shall be kept to gether for the use of my wife Elizabeth Wright during her life, and after her Dec.e to be divided as before mentioned. And lastly I make and ordain constitute & appoint my son James Wright my execu.r and my

two daughters Mary & Rosamond Wright my Executx. of this my last will and testament hereby revoking all former and other wills by me heretofore made declaring this to be my last.

. . . .

At a Court held for Fauquier County the 27th day of February 1792. This will was proved by the oaths of George Maddux and William Kerns witnesses thereto and ordered to be recorded.

And on the motion of James Wright the executor therein named who made oath and together with Thomas Keith his security entered into and acknowledged bond in the penalty of one thousand pounds conditioned as the law directs Certificate is granted him for obtaining a probate thereof in due form.

> Teste:
> H. Brooke, C.C."

This record indicates that John Wright died between June 1, 1785, and February 27, 1792, and probably sometime in early 1792, and identifies his family as follows:

Wife: Elizabeth (_____) Wright,

Children:
1) James Wright,
2) Mary Wright,
3) Rosamond Wright,
4) William Wright,
5) John Wright, and
6) Elizabeth (Wright) Parlow,

Grandchild, child of James Wright:
1) Betsey Wright

This record not only identifies one of the sons of 1792 John Wright of Fauquier County as a William Wright, but indicates that John Wright had gifted land to that son William Wright during his lifetime and that William Wright had sold that land before 1785. This is consistent with Fauquier County Deed M/169 in which John Wright gifted 185 acres of land to his son William Wright and, as will be set forth below, with the later sale of that land by William Wright and his wife Mary (_____) Wright by Fauquier County Deeds 1/369, 1/433, and 1/435 in 1762.

Part Two: William Wright, The Son Of 1792 John Wright, As Married To Mary _____

The identification of William Wright, the son of 1792 John Wright of Fauquier County, as married to a Mary _____ is based on a tracing of ownership of certain land in Prince William County and then later Fauquier County.

The will of Jonas Williams was dated on January 30, 1743/4, and probated on April 23, 1744, at Prince William County, Virginia, W.B. C/473 and gave to his son David Williams 111 acres of land adjacent to John Wright and appointed John Wright as executor with his wife Ann Williams:

> ". . . . I Jonas Williams Junr: of Prince William County . . . . do make and ordain this my last will . . . . Imprimis I give and bequeath to my beloved son David Williams one hundred and Eleven Acres of Land Joining to the land of John Wright gent. and the land of Simon Morgan, ... Lastly I Constitute and Appoint my well beloved wife Ann Williams Executrix and my beloved friend John Wright gent. Executor of this my last Will and Testament . . . . In Witness whereof I have set my hand seal this 30th day of January 1743/4
>
> . . . .
>
> At a Court held for the County of Prince William the 23d day of April 1744
>
> This will was presented in Court by Ann Williams one of the Executors therein named who made oath thereto and being proved by the oaths of Vincent Garner & John Lloyd two of the Witnesses thereto (who also made oath that they saw Elizabeth Sinclair the other Witness Subscribe her name as an Evidence) the said Will is admitted to Record and the said Ann having perform'd what the Laws require a Certificate is granted her for obtaining a probat thereof in due form
>
> Test.
> P Wagener Cl. Cur."

As set forth above, thereafter Anne (Darnall) Williams married Charles Garner and on July 22, 1748, at Prince William County, Virginia, D.B. L/44 and L/46 John Wright acquired 60 acres of land from Charles Garner and Ann (Darnall) (Williams) Garner, land which was part of a patent deed previously granted to Waugh Darnall and adjoining land which John Wright had previously purchased from Jonas Williams, Jr., and his wife Anne (Darnall) Williams.

As set forth above, on August 26, 1751, at Prince William County, Virginia, D.B. M/169 John Wright gave 185 acres of land to his son William Wright, and which included the 60 acres of Prince William Deeds L/44 and L/46.

On about August 26, 1762, at Fauquier County, Virginia, D.B. 1/369 William Wright and his wife Mary Wright sold 125 acres of land on which he then lived to Thomas Edwards:

"This Indenture made this _ day of ____ in the Year of our Lord One thousand seven Hundred and Sixty two Between William Wright and Mary his Wife of the Parish of Hamilton and County of Fauquier in the Colony of Virginia of the one part and Thomas Edwards of the Parish County and Colony aforesaid of the other part Witnesseth that the said William Wright and Mary his Wife . . . . sell unto the said Thomas Edwards . . . . a Certain Tract or Parcel of Land Containing one Hundred and Twenty five Acres it being the said Land whereon the said Wright now lives Adjoining to the Lands of Simon Morgan and Jonas Williams on the South side the Pignut Ridge and bounded as followeth (Vizt) Beginning at two Red oaks being the dividing Corner between the said Simon Morgan and Jonas Williams and Runs thence with the said Dividing Line S. 7-1/2° W. 130 poles to a Red oak a spanish Oak and Elm on a Branch thence North 83 degrees West 208 poles to a white oak Grub by two Red oak saplins on a hill in the old Line of the Deed thence with the line of the said Deed to the Beginning it being part of a Greater Dividend taken up by Waugh Darnall Decd by Patent Dated the 7th day of February 1725. . . .

Sign'd Sealed &	)	William Wright
delivered in	)	her
Presence of	)	Mary X Wright
Isaac Judd		mark
James Bashan		
Thomas Coleman		

At a Court held for Fauquier County the 26th Day of August 1762.

This Indenture was acknowledged by William Wright and Mary his Wife (she being first privily examined as the Law directs, to be their Act and Deed and Ordered to be recorded

Teste
H Brooke

The description of the land as part of a greater dividend taken up by Waugh Darnall indicates that this was the same land acquired by John Wright and part of the 185 acres of land gifted by John Wright to his son William Wright.

On October 13, 1762, at Fauquier County, Virginia, D.B. 1/433 and 1/435 William Wright and Mary Wright and David Williams and Betty Williams sold 60 acres of land, part of a tract taken up by Waugh Darnall, to John Waddle:

> "This Indenture made the 13th day of October in the Year of our Lord one thousand Seven Hundred & Sixty two . . . . Between William Wright and Mary his Wife and David Williams and Betty his Wife of the Parish of Hamilton and County of Fauquier of the one part and John Waddle of the same parish and County of the other part Witnesseth that the said William Wright and David Williams . . . . Sold unto the said John Waddle . . . . Sixty Acres of Land lying and being in the above said parish and County and Bounded as followeth Vizt Beginning at two Spanish Oaks thence So. 5○ Wt. 46 poles to a Box oak in a branch thence No. 84○ Wt. 220 poles to a Chesnut Oak on the Side of the Pignut Ridge thence No. 31○ Et. 46 poles to a white oak Grub thence Et. 187 poles to the beginning in Simon Morgans line being part of a Tract taken up by Waugh Darnall Decd Containing Sixty Acres
>
> . . . .
>
> | Sealed and Delivered |) | William Wright |
> |---|---|---|
> | In Presence of |) | her |
> | Simon Morgan | | Mary   X   Wright |
> | Thomas Carter | | mark |
> | William Norriss | | David Williams |
> | Charles Morgan | | |
> | Thomas Grubbs | | |
>
> At a Court Continued and held for Fauquier County the 25th Day of March 1763
>
> This Indenture was proved by the Oaths of Simon Morgan, William Norriss and Charles Moran jun Witnesses thereto to be the Act and Deed of the said William Wright & Mary his Wife & David Williams & Ordered to be recorded
>
> Teste
> H Brooke CC"

The reference to Waugh Darnall identifies this as the same land as that sold to John Wright by Charles Garner and his wife Ann (Darnall) (Williams) Garner and by John Wright given to his son William Wright.

Fauquier County Deeds 1/369, 1/433, and 1/435 show that William Wright, the son of John Wright, was old enough to receive land by gift from his father in 1751 and that he had a wife Mary (_____) Wright in 1762. Roger Morris was the first to explain the joinder of David and Betty Williams in Deeds 1/433 and 1/435. Their joinder as grantors in those deeds was necessitated by the prior sale of this land by Charles and Ann (Darnall) (Williams) Garner to John Wright. The land had been left by Jonas Williams, Jr., in his will to his son David Williams, not to David's mother Ann. Ann (Darnall) (Williams) Garner and her second husband Charles Garner sold the land without court approval to John Wright. Ann (Darnall) (Williams) Garner, even though executrix of the will of Jonas Williams, Jr., did not have authority to convey title to that land. Without David Williams' joinder in Deeds 1/433 and 1/435, there would have been a cloud on the title in the buyer John Waddle's hands.

A second and related explanation is drawn from language in Deed L/44 which refers to the land as "Joyning to the sd. John Wrights land wh he formerly purchased of Jonas Williams Junr & the sd Anne relation being had to the records of the aforesaid County of Prince William will more fully appear." There is no recorded deed from Williams to Wright in the Prince William County records before 1748. The language in the deed may indicate that Jonas Williams, Jr., and his wife Anne Williams had sold the same land to John Wright previous to Jonas Williams' death, but no deed was recorded, and the conveyance by Charles Garner and Anne (Darnall) (Williams) Garner for "five shilllings" was simply to complete the transfer to John Wright by recording a deed. But the gift of the same land to David Williams by Jonas Williams' will would have created a cloud on title. To remove that cloud for the buyer John Waddle, David Williams had to join in the deed by William and Mary Wright after he had become an adult.

Both explanations provide a reason for the joinder of David and Betty Williams in the deed.

Part Three: Mary (Grant) Wright As The Wife Of William Wright, The Son Of 1792 John Wright Of Fauquier County

The identification of Mary (Grant) Wright as the wife of a William Wright of Prince William and Fauquier Counties requires a review of the Grant family records.

The will of William Grant, Sr., dated January 24, 1726/7, and a codicil thereto dated January 4, 1733/4, was probated on February 1, 1733, at King George County, Virginia, W.B. A-1/98 and provided as follows:

". . . . I William Grant of the Parish of Sittenburn in the County of King George . . . . Do make & ordain this my last will . . . . Item I give & bequeath all the plantation & Land whereon I now dwell to my Son William Grant & his heirs forever . . . . what is not willed to be divided amongst my three Sons John William & Daniel also if any debts come against me or my estate for my three Sons John William & Daniel to pay it in equall part of payment Item I give unto my wife Also one shilling sterling she being eloped from me & her basely abusing of me . . . . As Witness my hand & Seal this 24th of Jany 1726/7

```
Sealed & Delivered                      his
in the presence of        William       M      Grant
Francis Etteridge                       mark
Thos Stribling
          his
John  X  Caddell
          mark
```

At a Court held for King George County the 1st day of Feby 1733

The last Will & Testament of William Grant deced was presented into Court by John Grant & Daniel Grant who made Oath thereto & the Same was proved by the Oath of Thomas Stribling one of the Witnesses thereto who also made Oath he saw Francis Etteridge another of the Witnesses evidence the Same which is admitted to record

                              Copa Teste
                              T. Turtner Cl Cur

Jany the 4th 1733/4

The last Will & Testament of William Grant my Will is that the labour of my two Negroes Jenny & Sarah shall be for the maintainance of my Son Willim Grants two Children

. . . .

At a Court held for King George County the 1st day of Feb 1733

Anthony Carnaby presented the above Nuncupative Codicil into Court & made Oath that the deced William Grant desired him to take notice thereof & the Same was ordered to go with the Will & to be admitted to record

Copa Teste
T Turner Cl Cur"

The will of William Grant, Jr., was probated on May 4, 1733, at King George

County, Virginia, W.B. A/98 and provided as follows:

". . . . I William Grant Junr . . . . my will & desire is that after my debts are __ that my well beloved wife Mary Grant Should enjoy all my whole Esta__ both real & personal during her widdowhood & my desire after if my wife should marry again that my brother John Grant Should take my two Children & take care of them untill they come to the age of eighteen & that my Estate be equally divided between my two Children Eliza & Mary I appoint my beloved wife Mary Grant & my brother John Grant my sole Executors Witness my hand & Seal

Test		his		
Charles Dean	William	I	Grant
John Brisroe		mark		

At a Court held for King George County the 4th day of May 1733

The last Will & Testament of William Grant was presented into Court by Mary Grant his Widow & John Grant his Executors who made oath thereto & the same was proved by the Oath of Charles Dean & admitted to record

Copa Test:
T. Turner Cl Cur"

King George County, Virginia, Will Book A-1 1721-1752 And Miscellaneous

Notes stated that:

"Grant, William [Junior] (d.t., 1732). William Grant, Jr. (c. 1707-1732) was murdered late in 1732; there are some particulars in COB#1, p. 626-628 and in COB#1, p. 635, 4 May 1733, it is noted that his widow, Mary Grant, presented his will in court but declared she would not accept the provisions made for her in the said testament, however, she accepted the executorship of the said will and on the same day entered into bond with John Grant, William Grant and Charles Deane, her securities [BB#1, p. 31b]. An inventory of the estate of William Grant, Jr., deceased, was returned to court on 1 June 1733 and recorded in I#1,

27

p. 161. It appears the widow Mary (_____) Grant shortly drops from the records and John Grant (c. 1704-1762) became the acting executor and guardian of Elizabeth Grant and Mary Grant only children and infant daughters of William Grant, Jr., deceased. In this capacity he filed detailed accounts in Fiduciary Account Book #3, pages 18-28, 1738-1746, showing disbursements for various items for the two girls including their board &c: By 2 December 1743 Elizabeth Grant, the elder daughter, had married (as his first wife) Anderson Doniphan, Gentleman, (c. 1720-1761) and shortly thereafter Mary Grant, the younger daughter, married William Wright of Prince William County and he was gentleman justice there in 1746."

On September 4, 1751, at King George County, Virginia, D.B. 1743-1752/442 & 443 William Wright and Mary his wife conveyed to Jane Payne one moiety of 180 acres of land given by the will of William Grant the Elder to his son William Grant the Younger, who was the father of Mary Wright:

"This Indenture made the fourth day of September . . . . one Thousand Seven hundred and Fifty one Between William Wright of the Parish of Hammilton in the County of Prince Wm of the one part and Jane Payne of the Parish of Hanover in the County of King George of the other part Witnesseth that the said William Wright . . . . Sell unto the said Jane Payne . . . . one certain Tract Piece or Parcel of Land and Premises, lying and being in the Parish of Hanover in the County of King George aforesaid Containing by Estimation Ninety Acres be the same more or less, it being one Moiety of one hundred & Eighty Acres of Land Given and Devised by the last Will and Testament of William Grant the Elder deced. to his son William Grant the Younger (who was the Father of the said Mary Wright party to these Presents) And by his Last Will did Devise the same together with his Personal Estate to be equally divided between his two Daughter's vizt. the aforesaid Mary & Elizabeth Grant, ... by Indenture Intended to be made between the said William Wright & Mary his wife on the one part and the said Jane Payne on the other part and to bear date the day next after the date of these Presents In Witness whereof the sd. William Wright to this present Indenture hath set his hand & Seale the day Month & Year first above written

Sealed and Delivered   )   William Wright
In the presence of   )
Wm. Bruce
John Grant
David Bronaugh

At a Court held for King George County on Thursday Sept. the 5" 1751. Then came William Wright personally into Court and Acknowledged this his Lease to Jane Payne which was admitted to Record

Copa. Test.
Harry Turner C.C."

King George County Deeds 1743-52/442 and 1743-52/444 clearly identify Mary Grant as married to a William Wright by 1751 and that that William Wright was then residing in Hamilton Parish, Prince William County.

Fauquier County was formed from Prince William County in 1759 and Hamilton Parish became part of that new county. The implication is clear that the William and Mary Wright of Fauquier County Deeds 1/369, 1/433, and 1/435 were the same William and Mary Wright of King George County Deeds 1743-52/442 and 1743-52/444, and, therefore, that William Wright, the son of 1792 John Wright of Fauquier County, was married to Mary (Grant) Wright and that they had married before 1751.

Part Four: William Wright Who Married Mary (Brent) Wright As Not The Son Of 1792 John Wright Of Fauquier County

There was a second William Wright with a wife Mary and connections to Fauquier County who needs to be distinguished from William Wright with a wife Mary who was the son of 1792 John Wright of Fauquier County.

The Register Of Overwharton Parish, Stafford County, Virginia, 1723-1758 And Sundry Historical And Genealogical Notes, compiled by George Harrison and Sanford King, listed the following records:

"B.   Wright, John son of William and Rosamond Wright, August 3, 1735.[2]

B.   Wright, Betty daughter of William and Rosamond Wright, September 10, 1737.

B.   Wright, Constant daughter of William and Rosamond Wright, September 7, 1739.

B.   Wright, Winfield child of William and Rose Wright, March 22, 1742.

B.   Wright, Mary daughter of William and Rosamond Wright, February 10, 1746.

D.   Wright, Rosanna wife of William Wright, march 16, 1753.

M.   Wright, William and Mary Brent, October 18, 1753.

2 - On October 14, 1700 at Stafford County court before John Washington, Gentleman Justice, Dade Massey, aged 21, and William Garner, aged 20, deposed that on October 10, 1700 they were at the house of Captain Richard Fossaker in Saint Paul's Parish where Richard Wright lay upon his death bed and he said it was his will that Mary Ellis have his son William and Gilbert Alsop have his son Richard and that Alsop should administer upon his estate. Gilbert Alsop acted as Wright's administrator and returned an inventory of it on April 8, 1701. William Wright (circa 1700-1789) married Rosamond [Rosanna], surname unknown, and the births of their five children are of record in The Register of Overwharton Parish. After her death on March 16, 1753, William Wright married Mary Brent on October 18, 1753; she predeceased him. In his old age he moved to Fredericksburg and the Virginia Herald of October 15, 1789 announced his death: "Died: On Monday last, Mr. William Wright, aged 89 years." His last will and Testament remains of record. The children of William and Rosamond [Rosanna] Wright were: I. John (August 3, 1735-May 11, 1791) married on June 5, 1755 Rosamond Grant (June 10, 1733-June 10, 1799), daughter of Captain John Grant (circa 1704-June 25, 1762) and Margaret Bronough (17 -March 11, 1756), his first wife, of King George County. John Wright was inspector of tobacco at the time of his death in Spotsylvania County; by will he bequeathed property in Spotsylvania and Culpeper [later Madison] counties. . . . ."

This record makes clear that even though 1789 William Wright had a wife Mary, he could not have been the son of 1792 John Wright of Fauquier County. As set forth above, 1792 John Wright was born before October 2, 1700, or about 1700. 1789 William Wright of Spotsylvania County was 89 years old at his death in 1789 and, therefore, was born in about 1700. The birth of 1789 William Wright of Spotsylvania County at nearly the same time as 1792 John Wright of Fauquier County means that 1789 William could not have been the son of 1792 John.

There are four other documents in Fauquier and Prince William Counties which relate to 1789 William Wright of Spotsylvania County that connect him with those counties and need to be distinguished from documents relating to William Wright, the son of 1792 John Wright of Fauquier County.

The first document is Fauquier County Deed 1/165. On September 25, 1760, at Fauquier County, Virginia, D.B. 1/165 William Wright leased 200 acres of land from Thomas Lord Fairfax for the life of himself, his wife Mary, and his son John:

> "This Indenture made this twenty fifth Day of September Anno Domini One thousand seven hundred and sixty Between the Right Honourable Thomas Lord Fairfax Baron of Cameron in that part of Great Britain called Scotland Proprietor of the Northern Neck of Virginia of the one part and William Wright of the County of Fauquier of the Colony of Virginia of the other part Witnesseth that the said Thomas Lord Fairfax . . . . to Farm Lett unto the said William Wright one Messuage Tenement and parcel of Land situate lying and being in the County of Fauquier being part of that Tract or parcel of Land called and known by the Name of the Manor of Leeds . . . . Containing two hundred Acres . . . . unto the said William Wright for and during the natural Life of him the said William Wright and for and during the natural Lives of Mary Wright his Wife and John Wright his Son and every of them longest living . . . ."

This record identifies William Wright as having a wife Mary Wright as the father of John Wright and indicates that John Wright was born before September 1760. This might be a record of William Wright and his wife Mary (Grant) Wright and would indicate that they had a son John Wright. However, it is more probable that this deed involved 1789 William Wright of Spotsylvania County, his wife Mary (Brent) Wright, and 1789 William Wright's son 1791 John Wright of Spotsylvania County.

As will be set forth below, 1809 William Wright of Franklin County was probably the son of 1792 John Wright of Fauquier County and 1809 William Wright probably had a son who was 1845 John Wright of Franklin County and who was born in 1747 or 1749 at Fauquier County. If Fauquier County Deed 1/165 involved 1809 William Wright of Franklin County, then he would have been acquiring land for a son who was only 11 or 13 years old. While not impossible, this is unlikely. In addition, 1809 William Wright left Fauquier County by January 28, 1764, and it would be unlikely that he would have left the county without disposing of his leasehold interest in that land, but there is no disposition of that land in the Fauquier County records.

The more likely identification of the William Wright of Fauquier County Deed 1/165 is that it was 1789 William Wright of Spotsylvania. Mary (Brent) Wright was 1789 William's second wife of seven years and his son John Wright was 25 years old in

1760. The lease measured by life estates of William, Mary, and John makes more sense for a family of adults than for family with a minor son. There would be no record of the disposition of this leasehold interest, because Mary (Brent) Wright predeceased her husband, William Wright died in 1789, and William's son John Wright died in 1791. The three life estates would have been completed in 1791 and by the terms of Deed 1/165 the leasehold right terminated and, therefore, no disposition of the lease would be required.

The second document is Fauquier County Deed 6/114. On August 9, 1775, at Fauquier County Deed 6/114 William Wright of Stafford County leased 40 acres of land to Feathergail Adams for farming:

> "This Indenture made this ninth day of August in the Year of our Lord one thousand seven hundred and seventy four Between William Wright of Stafford County of the one part and Feathergail Adams of the County of Fauquier of the other part Witnesseth that the said William Wright . . . . to farm let . . . . unto the said Feathergail Adams or his assigns all that tract of Land with the appurtenances situate lying and being in the said County of Fauquier now in the tenure and occupation of the said Feathergail Adams containing by survey about Forty acres and if there be more in the boundaries being bounded as followeth Beginning at a Chesnut Corner of John Hudnalls Land thence with the said Hudnalls line S 38 W 20 poles to a red Oak in said Hudnalls line then leaving his line S 58 E to a poplar in Wm Wrights land thence down a branch S 2 36° E to a Ash and white Oak between two branches near or in Charles Martins line thence with his line some Distance & runing to a supposed Corner to Hudnalls near a large spring now Corner to Mrs Bayhe a cross to the Beginning at the chesnut Corner . . . ."

The third document is Fauquier County Deed 12/387. On April 24, 1789, at Fauquier County, Virginia, D.B. 12/387 William Wright and John Wright and his wife Rosamond Wright sold 177 acres of land on Pignut Ridge which had been "taken up by John Hudnal:"

> "This Indenture made this twenty fourth day of April in the year of our Lord One thousand seven hundred and eighty nine Between William Wright, John Wright and Rosamond his wife of the County of Spotsylvania and state of Virginia of the one part and James Roach of the County of Prince William and state aforesaid of the other part Witnesseth that the said William Wright John Wright and Rosamond his wife do . . . . confirm unto the said James Roach his heirs and assigns forever A tract or parcel of Land situate lying and being in the County of Fauquier near the pignut Ridge containing one hundred and seventy seven

32

Acres bounded as follows Viz, Begining at a Stone marked IR Corner to Charles Martin (Deceased) thence with Martins line North forty three East two hundred and sixty seven poles to a red oak stump and small oak corner to Joseph Bailey thence with Bailey North fourteen West sixty two poles to a small white Oak by a red oak (down) by a spring thence South seventy five West one hundred poles to a chesnut Tree corner to Doctor Bells tract thence South thirty six West eighty three poles to a red oak and a gum thence south eighty six West forty two poles to a red oak thence South forty six West fifty eight poles to a white oak thence south sixteen West forty two poles to a Box oak corner to George Carters Land thence with Carters line south forty two East one hundred and fifteen poles to the Beginning it being a tract of Land taken up by John Hudnal . . . ."

The legal descriptions of Fauquier County Deeds 6/114 and 12/387 set forth above make clear that the same William Wright was involved in both transactions. Although the metes and bounds are not identical, Deed 6/114 refers to the land as adjacent to the land of William Wright, both deeds refer to the land as taken up by or adjacent to that of John Hudnall, both deeds refer to the land as adjacent to Charles Martin, and both deeds refer to the land as adjacent to Mrs. Bayle or Joseph Bailey. The listing of John Wright's wife as Rosamond Wright identifies this deed as by 1789 William Wright of Spotsylvania County, whose son 1791 John Wright of Spotsylvania County had married Rosamond Grant, as set forth above in The Register Of Overwharton Parish.

The fourth document is Prince William County Deed G/119. Fauquier County, Virginia, Deed records do not include a deed from John Hudnal to William Wright. However, the Index of Deeds for Prince William County lists Deed G/119 dated in 1744 from Hudnall to Wright. This is the only deed from a Hudnall to a Wright in the Prince William Index of Deeds. Deed Book G is missing from the county records, so a copy of this deed is unavailable, but the listing in the Index indicates that William Wright had acquired the land of Fauquier County Deed 12/389 in 1744 when the land was still part of the jurisdiction of Prince William County. And that in turn indicates that 1789 William Wright of Spotsylvania County had connections with Prince William and Fauquier Counties from 1744 to 1789, a period inclusive of Fauquier County Deed 1/165 dated in 1760 and reinforces the identification of 1789 William Wright of Spotsylvania County as the William Wright of Fauquier County Deed 1/165.

Part Five: The Identification Of 1805 William Wright Of Fauquier County As Not The Son Of 1792 John Wright Of Fauquier County

1805 William Wright of Fauquier County has been often identified as the son of 1792 John Wright of Fauquier County. All references that have been traced for this identification lead back to Charles Arthur Hoppin.

In his article "Some Descendants Of Richard Wright, Gentleman, Of Lond, England, And Northumberland, Virginia, 1655" in <u>Tyler's Quarterly Magazine</u>, Volume I, page 127, 1919, Charles Arthur Hoppin stated that the will of John Wright, Gent., dated June 1, 1785, named:

> ". . . . (6) - his son William Wright whose will, proved at Warrenton, April 28, 1806 [original will filed in the 1806 bundle in Fauquier count clerk's office], names wife Elizabeth, son William Wright, Jr., and refers to his other children without naming them; but on page 372 of Fauquier will book No. 8 is the entry of the division of the estate showing, to wit: "£974:18:4-1/2 - the sum to be divided between the fourteen children of the said Wm. Wright which will make each legatees part £69-12-8-3/4." Lack of space forbids the present citation of evidence upon these fourteen children, some of whom may be recognized in the following: Sarah, who had married the administrator of William Wright's estate, John Evans; Jane, who married Lain Smith; Mary, who married Joshua Lemert; David, who married Nancy Martin; Elijah, who married Polly Brannin; Joshua, who married Susan Carroll; Joseph, who married Elizabeth McCoy; Edward, who married Elizabeth Kay. [These marriage are recorded at Warrenton, Virginia.] William Wright, the said testator of 1805, served in Capt. Eustace's company, second Virginia regiment, in the War of the Revolution, as per a certificate recorded on page 442 of Fauquier court record book for March term, 1780. Circumspection must be observed in studying the numerous records of this William Wright, who had a stormy career as a litigant, lest he be confounded with the son of William of a Richard Wright* (wife Mary Ann), who died in Prince William county, 1767, this son William being the grantor of 1787 of lands in Prince William county to sons Zealy and John.
>
> *This Richard Wright was brother of William Wright, of Fredericksburg, Virginia, whose death is recorded in the Fredericksburg <u>Gazette</u> of October 15, 1789, viz.: "Died Monday last Mr Wm Wright, aged 89"; both were the orphaned sons of Richard Wright, who died, in 1700, in the house of Capt. Richard Fossaker in Stafford county, leaving a nuncupative will, in which Dade Massey deposes that Richard Wright "ye 10th day of Octor . . . . lay upon his death Bed & to ye best of his knowledge he heard him say that he will give his son William Wright to Mary Ellis & his son Richd Wright to Gilbert Alsop," etc. [Stafford county will book Z, page 57.]"

Mr. Hoppin apparently assumed that the William Wright named in 1792 John Wright's will was the same William Wright as the William whose will was probated in 1806 at Fauquier County, but no evidence was provided that connected those two William Wrights.

Mr. Hoppin repeated this identification in 1932 in his work The Washington Ancestry and Records of The McClain, Johnson, and Forty Other Colonial American Families:

> "Of the descendants of John[4] Wright, some of those from his osns William and James have been ascertained from the records, but it is the present purpose to portray in detail only the records of the family of his son John[5]. Thus the other children are now dismissed from notice beyond the following summary:. . . .

> William[5] Wright (senior) had a rather stormy career as a litigant, usually unsuccessful, in the county court. He married twice, Mary (____), and Elizabeth (____), who survived him. His military services are of record on page 25 of Volume I of Fauquier court minute books for September 27, 1759, his father then sitting as justice: "John Wright Present . . . John Cole, Elias Edmonds, William Wright, Armistead Churchill etc. Captains, took the usual oaths to his Majesty's person and Government and subscribed the Test." . . . . Also in Fauquier court minutes for March term 1780, p. 442, viz.: "A Certificate signed by Charles Mynn Thruston that William Wright, William Provo, Vincent Rollins, and Robert Sherington had served as soldiers in the last War [Revolution] in the second Virginia Regiment in Captain Eustace's Company was proved to be an authentic and true certificate by the oath of William Wright wh also made oath that no Claim or proof had ever before been made to land for the said services, which was ordered to be certified." The land presented to him on August 26, 1751, as stated in his father's will was 185 acres in the parish of Hamilton adjoining lands of Jonas Williams and Simon Morgan, "being part of a greater Dividant taken up by Waugh Darnall, Dec'd, by patent Dated the 17th day of February 1725." Of this land William Wright and wife Mary sold August 27, 1762, to Thomas Edwards, 125 acres; and with David Williams and wife Betty he sold the remaining 60 acres, on October 145, 162, to John Waddle. [Fauquier Deeds M-169 and L-371 and L-435.]

> This William Wright, Sr.'s will, proved April 28, 1806, names his (second) wife, Elizabeth, son William, Jr., (who married Elizabeth [____] and had eight children in the census of 1810), and refers to his other thirteen without giving their names or stating by which wife they were born; but on page 372 of Fauquier Will Book No. 8 is an entry of the division of his estate to wit: "£974:18:4-1/2 - the sum to be divided between the fourteen children of the said Wm Wright." Some of them

may be recognized from the marriage licenses and marriage returns recorded in the county clerk's office at Warrenton, ..."

Once again, Mr. Hoppin did not explain how he identified the William Wright who served in the Revolutionary War and whose will was probated in 1806 as the same William Wright who was the son of 1792 John Wright of Fauquier County and apparently assumed that both William Wrights were the same person. Mr. Hoppin stated that he was focused on the line of John Wright, the son of 1792 John Wright of Fauquier County, and offered only the summary quoted above regarding William Wright, the son of 1792 John Wright of Fauquier County.

In her book Major Francis Wright And Ann Washington With Allied Families, 1973, Anne Reed Ritchie stated that William Wright was a son of 1792 John Wright of Fauquier County and Elizabeth (Darnall) Wright, was born on November 28, 1740, at York County, Virginia, based on "Bible", or on November 1, 1740, based on "Patriot Index", married first Mary ____, but that this marriage was questionable, married second Elizabeth Lloyd on December 25, 1768, at York County, Virginia, died on August 29, 1805, at Fauquier County, Virginia, based on "Bible", or August 29, 1806, based on "Patriot Index", and was buried at Dermonte Burying Ground, Fauquier County, Virginia, and that 1805 William Wright of Fauquier County and Mary (____) Wright had two children and that 1805 William Wright of Fauquier County and Elizabeth (Lloyd) Wright had fourteen children. The location of the Bible record was not listed.

The Bible record referred to was probably the family record included with the documentation for the DAR Application #696077 of Eloise Wilma Ramsey Maynard, Shaker Heights, Cleveland, Ohio, which listed the following, all apparently in the same handwriting and written apparently at the same time:

"Family Record for William Wright

William Wright (my Father) was born in York County Virga. Novembr 1st 1740.

Elizabeth Wright, (his Wife, my Mother, & daughter of Wm Lloyd) was born below York Town near Hampton Virginia Novemr. the 7th 1750.

They married Decemr. the 25th 1768.

36

Wm Wright Decd. August 29th, 1806 near the upper end of Fauquier Co. at his own farm near the blue Ridge & was intered in Dermonts burying ground, near the spot his Mother was placed in, many years before; whose age when she Died was said to be upwards of 80 years.

Elizabeth Wright Decd. July 25. 1830. & was Intered at the same place.

William Wright, (son of Wm. & Elizth. Wright) was born in York Town Virginia Novemr. 10th 1769.

Amy Wright, (his wife Daughter of John & Martha Frazier was born in Chester Co, Pennsylvania Novemr. 1st 1778.

[List of children of William Wright and Amy (Frazier) Wright follows and is not included here]

[In a different handwriting from the part quoted above] William Wright Son of Willm and Elizabeth Wright Died august the 27th 1834 and . . . . [cut off on page]"

This family record prepared by 1805 William Wright's son had to have been made by that William Wright before his death on August 27, 1834, and apparently from information communicated to him by his parents. This family record that 1805 William Wright of Fauquier County was born on November 1, 1740, means that 1805 William Wright of Fauquier County could not have been the son of 1792 John Wright of Fauquier County.

As set forth above, in the gift deed from 1792 John Wright to his son William Wright dated August 26, 1751, at Prince William Deed M/169, William Wright was described as then residing on the land conveyed to him by his father John Wright:

". . . . for and in consideration of the natural love and affection which I have and Do bear unto my dear beloved son William Wright Do give grant and confirm and by these prsents do give grant and confirm unto the sd. William Wright all that messuage tract or parcel of Land which he now lives on containing one hundred and Eighty five acres Situate lying and being in the parish of hamilton and county of Prince William and Collony of Virginia . . . ."

1805 William Wright of Fauquier County was only 11 years old in 1751 and, therefore, could not be described as living on the land his father was giving to him. A different William Wright had to be involved.

In addition, as set forth above, William Wright, the son of 1792 John Wright of Fauquier County, and his wife Mary (Grant) Wright sold the land gifted to them in 1762 by Fauquier County, Virginia, Deeds 1/369, 1/433, and 1/435. William Wright of Hamilton Parish, Fauquier County (formerly Prince William County) and the husband of Mary (Grant) Wright was described in King George County Deed 1743-1752/442 as married to Mary Grant in 1751:

> "This Indenture made the fourth day of September . . . . in the year of our Lord God one Thousand Seven hundred and Fifty one Between William Wright of the Parish of Hammilton in the County of Prince Wm of the one part and Jane Payne of the Parish of Hanover in the County of King George of the other part Witnesseth that . . . . he the said Wm. Wright doth hereby . . . . Grant Bargain & Sell unto the said Jane Payne . . . . one certain Tract Piece or Parcel of Land and Premises, lying and being in the Parish of Hanover in the County of King George aforesaid Containing by Estimation Ninety Acres be the same more or less, it being one Moiety of one hundred & Eighty Acres of Land Given and Devised by the last Will and Testament of William Grant the Elder deced. to his son William Grant the Younger (who was the Father of the said Mary Wright party to these Presents) And by his Last Will did Devise the same together with his Personal Estate to be equally divided between his two Daughter's vizt. the aforesaid Mary & Elizabeth Grant,
> . . . ."

Once again, 1805 William Wright of Fauquier County would have been only 11 years old in 1751 and, therefore, could not have been the husband of Mary (Grant) Wright.

Charles Arthur Hoppin apparently did not have access to the Bible or family record referred to by Anne Reed Ritchie or he would have noted the anomaly of an 11 year old residing on and receiving a gift of land from his father.

In addition, the family record in DAR Application #696077 stated that 1805 William Wright was born at York County, Virginia, and that William Wright, the first child of 1805 William Wright and Elizabeth (Lloyd) Wright, was born on November 10, 1769, at Yorktown, Virginia. These two events are inconsistent with the residence of 1792 John Wright in the Prince William/Fauquier County area during this period and his son William Wright's presence there in 1751 when he resided on the land in Prince William Deed M/169 and William Wright's presence there in 1762 when Prince William Deed M/169 was delivered to him and his wife and the land then sold by them.

Ms. Ritchie further stated that William Wright and John Wright, sons of 1792 John Wright, both left the county of Fauquier, but that William Wright returned. The more logical explanation is that William Wright, the son of 1792 John Wright, did leave the county, but a second William Wright, the one born in 1740 in York County and married to Elizabeth Lloyd and in York County in 1769, moved into Fauquier County after the first William Wright had left and became confused with the first William Wright because of their identical names.

This is the likely explanation of the progression of these two William Wrights in Fauquier County, since in addition there are no deed records that connect 1805 William Wright of Fauquier County with 1792 John Wright of Fauquier County and the first deed that can be associated with 1805 William Wright was dated in 1780.

The first deed that can be clearly identified with 1805 William Wright is Fauquier County Deed 7/300 dated September 5, 1780, by which William Wright purchased 175 acres of land from Hezekiah and Henrietta Turner:

> "This Indenture made this twenty fifth day of September in the year of our Lord one thousand seven hundred and eighty Between Hezekiah Turner and Henrietta his Wife of Fauquier County and Common Wealth of Virginia of the one part and William Wright of the County and State aforesaid of the other part Witnesseth that the said Hezekiah Turner and Henrietta his wife . . . . make over unto the said William Wright his heirs and assigns forever All, that lott or parcell of land lying in Fauquier County Begining at a red oak a corner tree of Mr. George Adams and Cap. John Thomas Chunn, runing thence with the said George Adams line South ten and a half degrees west ninety two poles to a red oak marked HW thence south sixty degrees west fifty six poles to a red oak marked HW thence west thirty nine poles to a poplar marked HW thence north sixty degrees west twenty six poles to a white oak marked HW thence north thirty three degrees west twenty eight poles to a white oak marked HW thence north eleven degrees west one hundred and thirty poles to a Chesnut marked HW thence north twenty five degrees west forty poles to a Chesnut oak marked HW thence north seventy degrees east one hundred and sixteen poles to a white oak marked TC HW a corner tree of Cap John Thomas Chunns thence with Cap. Chunns line, south thirty degrees East one hundred and forty poles to the first Begining tree containing one hundred and seventy five acres of land
> . . . .

At a Court held for Fauquier County the 25th day of September 1780

This Indenture and the receipt thereon endorsed were acknowledged by the said Hezekiah Turner and Henrietta his Wife (She being first privily examined as the law directs) to be their act and deed and ordered to be recorded

Teste
H Brooke CC"

On April 7, 1794, at Fauquier County, D.B. 11/494 William Wright and his wife Elizabeth Wright sold the land purchased by Fauquier County Deed 7/300 to John Thomas Dean:

"This Indenture made this seventh April in the year of our Lord one thousand seven hundred and ninety four Between William Wright and Elizabeth his wife of Fauquier County and Commonwealth of Virginia of the one part and John Thomas Chunn of the County and State aforesaid of the other part Witnesseth that the said William Wright and Elizabeth his wife . . . . make over unto the said John Thomas Chunn . . . . all that Lott or parcel of Land lying in Fauquier County Begining at a red oak a corner tree of Mr George Adams and the said Chunn, running thence with the said George Adams's line South Ten and a half degrees West ninety two poles to a red oak marked HW, thence South Sixty degrees West fifty six poles to a red oak marked HW, thence West Thirty nine poles to a poplar marked HW, thence north Sixty degrees west twenty Six poles to a white oak marked HW, thence north thirty three degrees West twenty eight poles to a white oak marked HW, thence North eleven degrees West One hundred and thirty poles to a chesnut marked HW, thence North twenty five degrees West forty poles to a chesnut oak marked HW thence North Seventy degrees East one hundred and sixteen poles to a white oak marked TCHW corner tree of the said Chunns, thence with his Line South thirty degrees east One hundred and forty poles to the first Begining Containing one hundred and seventy five Acres being the same Land conveyed by Deed of Bargain and Sale from Hezekiah Turner and Henrietta his wife to the said William Wright bearing date the 25th day of September in the year 1780 and duly recorded in the County Court of Fauquier reference being thereunto had will more fully appear . . . ."

The reference in the legal description to the land being the same as that purchased on September 25, 1780, clearly identifies the William Wright of Fauquier Deed 7/300 as the same William Wright of Fauquier Deed 11/494 and the listing of William Wright's wife as Elizabeth identifies this William Wright as 1805 William Wright of Fauquier County whose wife was named in his will as Elizabeth.

Between October 14, 1762, when William Wright and his wife Mary Wright sold the land gifted to William by his father 1792 John Wright of Fauquier County by Fauquier Deed 1/433, and September 5, 1780, when 1805 William Wright of Fauquier County purchased 175 acres of land by Fauquier County Deed 7/300, there is only one deed naming a William Wright and that is Fauquier County Deed 6/114 dated August 9, 1775, by which William Wright of Stafford County leased 40 acres of land to Feathergail Adams for farming. As set forth above, that deed involved 1789 William Wright of Spotsylvania County and not 1805 William Wright of Fauquier County.

The result of the tracing of the Fauquier County deeds naming a William Wright is that there is no deed record connecting 1805 William Wright of Fauquier County to 1792 John Wright of Fauquier County, that the last clear deed record of William Wright, the son of 1792 John Wright of Fauquier County, was dated October 14, 1762, that 1805 William Wright of Fauquier County first appeared in the land records of Fauquier County on September 25, 1780, when he purchased 175 acres of land by Fauquier County Deed 7/300, and that during the gap in time from 1762 to 1780 only one deed record of a William Wright appears and that is Fauquier County Deed 6/114 involving 1789 William Wright of Spotsylvania County.

The conclusion to be drawn from the deed evidence set forth above is that William Wright, the son of 1792 John Wright of Fauquier County, sold the land given to him by his father in 1762 and left Fauquier County, as his brother John Wright later did also, and that 1805 William Wright of Fauquier County moved to Fauquier County from York County by 1780 when he first purchased land.

Based on the evidence set forth above, it is clear that 1805 William Wright of Fauquier County was not the son of 1792 John Wright of Fauquier County.

Part Six: Documentary Evidence Connecting 1809 William Wright Of Franklin County To Fauquier County

The first record of 1809 William Wright in Bedford County records (prior to the formation of Franklin County) is Bedford County, Virginia, Deed 3/276 dated May 24, 1768, in which William Wright acted as a witness to a deed from John Greer and Thomas Elliott to John Hall. On May 22, 1770, at Bedford County, Virginia, D.B. 4/443

William Wright acted as a witness to a deed from Justice Beech to Richard Brown for land on Maggotte Creek. And on November 14, 1772, at Bedford County, Virginia, W.B. 1/495 William Wright was named as executor of the will of John Miller and Mary Wright was a witness to the will. These records are chronologically consistent with 1792 John Wright's son William Wright sale of his land in Fauquier County in 1762, as will be set forth below, and his departure from that county by 1764.

This 1809 William Wright of Franklin County had a wife Mary (____) Wright, owned land on Maggotty Creek in a part of Bedford County which became Franklin County in 1785, and his will was dated on October 10, 1808, and probated on January 2, 1809, at Franklin County, Virginia, W.B. 1/368.

There are two documents which connect this 1809 William Wright of Franklin County to Fauquier County.

On September 24, 1759, at Fauquier County, Virginia, D.B. 1/65 William Wright and Timothy Stamps were both witnesses to a deed from James Scott to Thomas Stamps.

On about April 28, 1774, at Bedford County, Virginia, County Court Loose Papers Timothy Stamps filed a complaint for debt against "William Wright Black Smith" based on a judgment previously obtained in Fauquier County:

> "To the Worshipful the Court of Bedford County, Timothy Stamps humbly showeth, That William Wright Black Smith stands indebted to him in £1.7.0 122 w. Tobo. 15/ by former Judgment of Faquier Court and refuseth Payment: Wherefore your Petitioner prays Judgment against him for the same, with Costs.
>
> And shall pray, &c."

This record both identifies William Wright's prior residence in Fauquier County and his association with Timothy Stamps.

On April 28, 1774, at Bedford County, Virginia, County Court Loose Papers Timothy Stamps obtained a summons against William Wright Blacksmith to answer his complaint for debt and on August 30, 1778, at Bedford County, Virginia, County Court Loose Papers Timothy Stamps obtained another summons against William Wright Blacksmith to answer his complaint for debt.

The common identity of a Timothy Stamps in Fauquier County associated as a witness with William Wright in Fauquier County Deed 1/65 and as parties to a lawsuit in Bedford County (before the formation of Franklin County) on a judgment obtained in Fauquier County clearly ties 1809 William Wright of Franklin County to Fauquier County.

Part Seven: Similarity Of Handwriting

There are also three documents which contain the handwriting of William Wright, the son of 1792 John Wright of Fauquier County, and 1809 William Wright of Franklin County and a comparison of the handwriting in the three documents indicates they were all signed by the same person.

Genealogy Of John J. Wright Of Virginia, Indiana and Kansas by John Calvin Wright stated that there was a lawsuit for debt against William Wright in Fauquier County, Virginia, and:

> ". . . .a summons dated on the 28th day of January (or February, text not clear), 1764" to answer to a plea of debt for six pounds and one shilling current money-damage forty shillings."
>
> T. Brooke

> The original of a personal note given by William[5] Wright for the above debt is on file in the office of the Clerk of the Court at Warrenton. It is dated "29th day of August, 1763 and is a promise to pay "six pounds, one shilling current money on the 10th day of October next."

> On the back of the "Summons" appears this memoranda "Not found copy left etc. Orig. Young."

> The author made a photographic copy of these papers and obtained a facsimile of William[5] Wright's signature.
> 7. When the author began his study of his Wright ancestors family records easily carried him back to Franklin County, Virginia and to William Wright Senr. whose Will was probated on Jan. 2nd 1809. The original of this Will is on file at Rocky Mount in Franklin County (W.B. No. 1, p. 368.)

> Shortly before this writing the author sent the photographic copy of William Wright's signature mentioned in Item 6 to Mrs. Doris G. Dickinson engaged in genealogical research at Rocky Mount, Franklin Co., Va. and asked her to compare it with that on the Will. Under date of Aug. 22, 1941 the following reply was received:

"Dear Mr. Wright:

Mr. Carper (Clerk of the Court) and I compared the two signatures of William Wright and so far as we can see they are the same. There couldn't possibly be two different William Wrights with handwriting as much alike as in the said Will and the one you sent me. I would be willing to swear they are the same."

The promissory note referred to by John Calvin Wright has not as yet been located, so his and Ms. Dickinson's conclusion cannot be independently verified as to that note. But another document signed by William Wright in Fauquier County has been located. On February 28, 1761, at Fauquier County, Virginia, County Court Loose Papers William Wright executed a surety bond for 51£ 6S 2p to secure Peter Hon:

"Know all Men by these Presents, That I William Wright Junr of Fauquier County am held and firmly bound unto Peter Hon Esqr merchant in Whitehaven in the just and full Sum of Fifty One pounds six shillings & two pence Currt. money To be paid unto the said Peter Hon Esqr his certain Attorney, his Heirs, Executors, Administrators, or Assigns: To which Payment well and truly to be made, I bind myself, my Heirs, Executors, and Administrators, firmly by these Presents. Sealed with my Seal, and dated this Twenty Eigth Day of February Anno Dom. One Thousand Seven Hundred and Sixty One

The Condition of the above Obligation is such, That if the above bound William Wright do and shall well and truly pay, or cause to be paid, unto the said Peter Hon Esqr his certain Attorney, Executors, Administrators, or Asigns, the just Sum of Twenty five pounds Thirteen Shillings & one penny (like Currt. money) on demand Then the above Obligation to be void; or else to remain in full Force and Virtue.

                                          William Wright
Sealed and Delivered   )
in the Presnce   )
William Carr"

The designation "Junr" was probably to distinguish this William Wright from 1789 William Wright of Fredericksburg who was an older William Wright and, as set forth above, on September 25, 1760, by Fauquier County, Virginia, D.B. 1/165 had leased land in Fauquier County. A copy of that surety bond with the signature of William Wright, the son of 1792 John Wright, is attached.

Roger Morris obtained a copy of the original will of 1809 William Wright of Franklin County from the Franklin County Court where it is still on file. This is not the copy of the will made by the clerk when recording the will in the County Will Book. A copy of that original will with 1809 William Wright's signature is attached.

In addition, on September 3, 1790, at Franklin County, Virginia, Suit Papers, Virginia State Library, 1809 William Wright of Franklin County executed a promissory note to Henry Buford for £6, 12s. Henry Buford sued William Wright for payment and a faded copy of that note was included in loose court papers for the case. A copy of that promissory note with 1809 William Wright's signature is also attached.

KNOW all Men by these Presents, That I William Wright Junt of Fauquier County am held and firmly bound unto Peter Hon Esqr Merchant in Whitehaven in the just and full Sum of Fifty One pounds Six Shillings & two pence Curr. money To be paid unto the said Peter Hon Esqr his certain Attorn, his Heirs, Executors, Administrators, or Assigns: To which Payment well and truly to be made, I bind myself, my Heirs, Executors, and Administrators, firmly by these Presents. Sealed with my Seal, and dated this Twenty Eighth Day of February Anno Dom. One Thousand Seven Hundred at Sixty One

THE Condition of the above Obligation is such, That if the above bound William Wright do and shall well and duly pay, or cause to be paid, unto the said Peter Hon Esqr his certain Attorney, Executors, Administrators, or Assigns, the just Sum of Twenty five pounds Thirteen Shillings & One penny (like Curr. money) on demand Then the above Obligon to be void; or else to remain in full Force and Virtue.

Sealed and Deliv'd
in the Presence

William Cass

William Wright

In the name of god Amen ~~this~~ the 10 ~~Day~~ October 1808 —————

I William Wright, of franklin County ~~& City~~ am well in health and
Of perfect senses and Memory thanks be to god for his Mercies and
Caleng to mind the ~~Immortallity~~ Mortallity of man and that all men once
Must Die I Doe make constitute ordain and appoint this
My last will and testament in Manner and ~~~~
~ Form followith ————————

~~ Item I give and Bequeath unto my Grand Son Enoch Wright
All my land and plantation where I now live and all my ~~other~~ ~~~
~~~ tune and force To him and his heirs for Ever and then Enoch shall find ~~~
~~~ they sd William ~~shall find~~ with all things that ~~~~ ~~~~ during
His life I Likewise appoint my two sons James Wright and
George Wright and Enoch Wright my whole and sole
Executors and trustees of this my last will and testament

Witness my hand and Seal The Day and year
Above Written   Isaac Abshire
Witness - Philemon Smith   William Wright
          Abraham Abshire

The Common Wealth of Virginia to the sheriff of
Franklin County Greeting, You are hereby Commanded
to take William Wright Sen.
if he be found in your Bailiwick there safely keep so
that you have his Body before the Justices of our Court of
our said County at the Court house on the first Monday
in march next to answer Henry Buford of a Plea of Debt
for Six pound Twelve Shillings Damage 40/
And have then there this Writ Witness James Callaway
Clerk of our said County Court at the Court house on the 27
day of Decem.r 91 in the XVI year of the Common Wealth
            James Callaway Clk.

I promise to pay Henry Buford on or before
the tenth day of November next the Just and
full sum of six pounds Twelve shillings cur
rent money of Virginia to bear Interest from
the date hereof It being for Value received
Witness my Hand this third day of Septem.r
1790
£ 6. 12. .
Test.
Jubal Early
            William Wright

A comparison of the signature on the surety bond, the signature on the will of 1809 William Wright, and the signature on the promissory note indicates a strong similarity of handwriting and suggests that all three documents were signed by the same person and thereby supporting the identification of 1809 William Wright of Franklin County as the same person as William Wright, the son of 1792 John Wright of Fauquier County.

Part Eight: Family Naming Evidence Connecting Wright And Grant Families

There is family naming evidence that connects the family of 1809 William Wright of Franklin County to the Grant family and to the family of 1792 John Wright of Fauquier County.

One of the children of 1809 William Wright of Franklin County and Mary (_____) Wright named in his will was 1823 James Wright of Franklin County. 1823 James Wright of Franklin County named one of his sons James Grant Wright and that son named one of his sons James Grant Wright, Jr.

A second child of 1809 William Wright of Franklin County and Mary (_____) Wright was 1830 William Wright of Franklin County and one of 1830 William Wright's sons was 1857 James Wright of Delaware County, Indiana, who named one of his sons William Grant Wright.

The recurrence of the middle name Grant among the descendants of 1809 William Wright of Franklin County and Mary (_____) Wright indicates a family connection to the Grant family and suggests that William Wright's wife Mary was the Mary (Grant) Wright, daughter of William Grant, of the King George County deeds.

There is even similarity in the given names of the families. As will be set forth below, 1809 William Wright of Franklin County and Mary (_____) Wright had four and possibly five sons: probably 1845 John Wright of Franklin County, possibly Wingfield Wright, 1823 James Wright of Franklin County, 1830 William Wright of Franklin County, and 1843 George Wright of Franklin County. As set forth above, 1792 John Wright of Fauquier County and Elizabeth (Bronaugh) (Darnell) Wright had three sons: John, William, and James. As set forth above, William Grant, Jr., had only two daughters, but his undated will was probated on May 4, 1733, at King George County, Virginia, W.B. A-1/98 and appointed his brother John Grant as executor. The will of William's father

William Grant, Sr., was dated on January 24, 1726/7, a codicil thereto was dated on January 4, 1733/4, both were probated on February 1, 1733/4, at King George County, Virginia, W.B. A-1/101, and listed three sons: William, John, and Daniel. John Grant married Margaret Bronaugh, daughter of Jeremiah Bronaugh and sister of Elizabeth (Bronaugh) (Darnell) Wright. On July 7, 1757, at King George County, Virginia, D.B. 4/280 John Grant deeded his estate, subject to a retained life estate, to his children, including his sons John, Daniel, George, and William. A comparison of naming patterns shows the similarity among these four families:

1809 William Wright & Mary (Grant) Wright	1792 John Wright & Elizabeth (Bronaugh) (Darnell) Wright	William Grant, Sr. & Elizabeth (____) Grant	John Grant & Margaret (Bronaugh) Grant
John	John	John	John
William	William	William	William
James	James		
George			George
		Daniel	Daniel

Part Nine: Suggestive Evidence Regarding 1809 William Wright of Franklin County And 1845 John Wright Of Franklin County

There is additional suggestive evidence regarding 1809 William Wright of Franklin County and his probable son 1845 John Wright of Franklin County.

Fauquier County, Virginia, D.B. 1/165 dated September 25, 1760, listed the lessees as William Wright, his wife Mary Wright, and their son John Wright, but as set forth above, this deed probably involved 1789 William Wright of Spotsylvania County and 1791 John Wright of Spotsylvania County, not William Wright, the son of 1792 John Wright of Fauquier County.

On October 1, 1832, at Pension File S6449 John Wright filed an application for a pension for his services in the Revolutionary War:

"State of Virginia Franklin county Sct,

On this day to wit 1st of october 1832 personally appeared in open court before the court of Franklin county now siting John Wright a resident of Franklin County & state of Virginia born in Fauquier Va and aged 85(?) years who being first duly sworn according to Law doth on his oath make the following declaration in order to obtain the benefit of the act of Congress passed 7th June 1832 That he entered the service of the united States under the following officers during the revolution war and served as is herein Stated That early in the revolution war, he entered voluntarily in a company called minute men who had pledged to take the field when required which company was commanded by Captain Moses Greer whose affidavit he here files - . . . . He enroled himself in Capt Greers company in Bedford county Va where he then resided and in the foregoing tours marched invariably from that county and all ways continued in service till discharged. . . . . he has resided since the war in Franklin County Virginia . . . ."

The age is difficult to read and may have been 83 years, rather than 85 years, indicating a date of birth in about 1747 or 1749. A pension of $30 per year was granted, but the termination date by reason of John Wright's death was not listed in the file:

"Virginia

John Wright of Franklin in the State of Va who was a pr: in the compy commanded by Captain Greer of the Regt commanded by Col: Callaway in the Va: line for 9 months from 1778.

Inscribed on the Roll of Virginia at the rate of 30 Dollars _ Cents per annum, to commence on the 4th day of March 1831.

Certificate of Pension issued the 17th day of Jan" 33 and __ 19 next

H. Claiborne House of Reps

Arrears to 4th of Sept 1832	45.-
Semi=anl allowance ending 4 Mar 33	15.-
	$60.-

Revolutionary Claim
Act June 7, 1832

Recorded by Matthew Rice Clerk, Book D Vol. 7 Page 120

1881 May 21 Hon Eppa Hanton-referring him to 3d Auditor for date to which last paid"

In <u>Genealogy Of John J. Wright Of Virginia, Indiana and Kansas</u> the author John Calvin Wright included the following letter:

"General Accounting Office
Washington

Reconciliation and
Clearance Division
In reply please quote
RC-37002-JM
148530   April 7, 1941

Mr. J. C. Wright
5624 Western Avenue,
Chevy Chase, Maryland.

Sir:

In reply to your letter of February 3, 1941, in which you request information concerning John Wright, Certificate No. 4310, Virginia Agency, a pensioner of the Revolutionary War, you are advised the records of this office show that the last payment of pension, covering the period from March 4, 1844 to September 4, 1844, was made at Richmond, Virginia, on January 11, 1845, to Elisha K. Gilbert, as attorney for the pensioner. On December 16, 1844, the pensioner certified that he had resided in Franklin County, Virginia, for sixty years, and that prior thereto, he resided in Fauquier County, Virginia.

No further information has been found of record in this office.

Respectfully,

P. D. Fallon
Asst. Chief, Reconciliation and Clearance Division."

This record indicates that John Wright survived until at least December 16, 1844, and probably until January 11, 1845.

On April 14, 1845, at Franklin County, Virginia, Chancery Court Loose Papers, Reel 157/108, John Gearhart filed a notice of taking deposition of Otey Forbes that stated that Ezekiel Wright was administrator of the estate of John Wright, Sr.:

"To Mr. Ezekeil Wright (Admr of John Wright Sr Decd)

Sir, Take notice, ... wherein you the said Ezekiel Wright Administrator of John Wright Sr decd is plaintiff and I am defendant; . . . . Given under my hand this 14 day of April 1845

John Gearhart"

This record indicates that John Wright had died by April 14, 1845, and this John Wright is identified as 1845 John Wright of Franklin County.

1845 John Wright of Franklin County resided near 1809 William Wright of Franklin County and his wife Mary (_____) Wright in Franklin County. As set forth above, in Pension File S6449, 1845 John Wright of Franklin County stated that he was born in Fauquier County and was 85 or possibly 83 years old, indicating a date of birth in about 1747 or 1749, and that he resided in Bedford County at the time of enlistment for service in the Revolutionary War, and had resided in Franklin County since the War. The combination of the birth of 1845 John Wright in Fauquier County, his birth in 1747 or 1749 which is consistent with the marriage of William Wright and Mary (Grant) Wright by 1751, and the proximity of 1845 John Wright to the family of 1809 William Wright in Franklin County indicates that 1845 John Wright of Franklin County was probably the son of 1809 William Wright of Franklin County and Mary (_____) Wright.

The 1786 Personal Property Tax List for Franklin County, Virginia, listed five Wrights who can be identified as 1809 William Wright of Franklin County, his sons 1823 James Wright of Franklin County, 1830 William Wright of Franklin County, and 1843 George Wright of Franklin County, as well as 1845 John Wright of Franklin County. This is suggestive that there was only one Wright family in Franklin County that year and that 1845 John Wright was a fourth son of 1809 William Wright. The 1787, 1788, and 1789 Personal Property Tax Lists for Franklin County, Virginia, similarly list the five Wrights named above as well as 1849 Thomas Wright of Franklin County and 1844 Joseph Wright of Hardin County, Kentucky, two sons of 1815 Joseph Wright of Bedford County and grandsons of 1763 Thomas Wright of Bedford County. These records reinforce the impression that 1845 John Wright was a son of 1809 William Wright.

The will of 1809 William Wright was dated on October 10, 1808, probated on January 2, 1809, at Franklin County, Virginia, W.B. 1/368, and provided as follows:

".... October the 10th Day 1808 I William Wright of Franklin County .... I Doe make constitute ordain and appoint this my last Will and testament in manner and Form followeth - Item I give and Bequeath unto my Grand Son Enoch Wright all my land and plantation where I now live and all my stock and firneture To him and his heirs for Ever and the sd. Enoch shall find the sd. William with all things that is Needs full During His life I Likewise appoint my two sons James Wright and George Wright and Enoch Wright my whole and Sole Executors and trustees of this my Last Will and Testament Witness my hand and Seal the day and year above written

Witness   William Wright
Isaac Abshire
Philemon Smith
Abraham Abshire

At a Court held for Franklin County January 2d 1809

This last Will and Testament of William Wright deceased was proved by the oath of Isaac Abshire Philemon Smith & Abraham Abshire the witnesses hereto, and ordered to be recorded.

And at a Court held for Franklin County September 3d 1810, on the motion of George Wright one of the executors herein named, who took the oath prescribed by Law and together with James Wray his security entered into and acknowledged his bond in the penalty of fifty Dollars, conditioned according to Law, Certificate is granted him for obtaining a Probat in due form, liberty being reserved to the other Executors in the said Will named to join in the Probat when they shall think fit.

Teste,
Jas Callaway CFC"

Although 1809 William Wright did not list a John Wright as one of his children, the listing of Enoch Wright as a grandson of 1809 William Wright indicates that he had an unnamed son who was the father of Enoch. The children of 1809 William Wright's sons 1823 James Wright of Franklin County, 1830 William Wright of Franklin County, and 1843 George Wright of Franklin County have been identified and none is an Enoch Wright. The result is that 1809 William Wright had at least one other son and that would probably have been 1845 John Wright of Franklin County. However, it is possible that there was another son who had predeceased 1809 William and, therefore, the identification of Enoch Wright as a son of 1845 John Wright of Franklin County remains uncertain. For example, the 1790 Personal Property Tax List for Franklin County, Virginia, listed a Winkfield Wright who might have been a son of 1809 William Wright. If Enoch Wright can ever be identified as the son of a John Wright, then the identification of 1845 John Wright of Franklin County as a son of 1809 William Wright of Franklin County will be confirmed and that would be further confirmation of the identification of 1809 William Wright of Franklin County as a son of 1792 John Wright of Fauquier County.

There is a Family Bible of Thomas Houston that is held by the Virginia Historical Society and attached to the Bible record are the notes of William E. Pullen which stated:

> "Bible of Thomas Huston of Franklin County, Virginia, and taken by him to Union County, Indiana and inherited by his daughter, Sarah [Huston] Wright. Given to Virginia Historical Society by Sarah's great-great grand-daughter, Imogene Barker [Mrs. William E.] Pullen 1969.
>
> . . . .
>
> Sarah Huston, born Aug. 26, 1813, Franklin married cousin Matthew Wright, Union County, Indiana, Oct. 18, 1841 and died in Hamilton County, Indiana, March 27, 1887.
>
> See Wright Bible in Historical Society."

As will be set forth below, Sarah (Huston) Wright was a daughter of Thomas Huston and Tabitha (Wright) Huston and granddaughter of 1845 John Wright of Franklin County and Mary (Wray) Wright. Matthew W. Wright was a son of 1839 John A. Wright of Franklin County and Elizabeth (Abshire) Wright, grandson of 1830 William Wright of Franklin County and Catherine (Doran) Wright, and great grandson of 1809 William Wright of Franklin County and Mary (_____) Wright. Sarah Huston and Matthew W. Wright would be cousins if 1845 John Wright of Franklin County was a son of 1809 William Wright of Franklin County. However, Mr. Pullen did not indicate what the source was for identifying Sarah and Matthew as cousins and further research will be required to confirm the accuracy of that statement. If this statement of cousinship can

55

be confirmed, then again the identification of 1845 John Wright of Franklin County as a son of 1809 William Wright of Franklin County will be confirmed and the identification of 1809 William Wright of Franklin County as a son of 1792 John Wright of Fauquier County will be further confirmed.

Substantial research has been undertaken to resolve the two open issues discussed above and I would much appreciate any assistance which readers of this article may provide to identify the name of the father of Enoch Wright and to confirm the cousinship of Matthew W. Wright and Sarah (Huston) Wright. Enoch Wright married Susannah Abshire, resided in Preble County, Ohio, Elkhart County, Indiana, Tulare County, California, and Fresno County, California, and died probably between 1871 and 1878 at California, probably at Fresno County. Matthew W. Wright died on February 20, 1865, at Hamilton County, Indiana, and Sarah (Huston) Wright died on March 22, 1887, at Hamilton County, Indiana.

Part Ten: Contrary Identifications of 1792 John Wright's Son William Wright

There have been two other identifications of 1792 John Wright's son William Wright that differ from the above analysis.

First Alternative: William Wright Who Married Mary Williams

The first alternative identification is that the William Wright who married Mary Williams was the son of 1792 John Wright of Fauquier County.

DAR Application #388187 for Genevieve (Wright) Smith dated February 24, 1949, stated that William Wright was a son of John Wright and Elizabeth (Darnall?) Wright, was born in 1727 or 1728 at Dumfries, Prince William County, Virginia, married Mary Williams in 1746 or 1747, resided in Prince William County, Virginia, in the part which became Fauquier County, and died in 1808 at Boone Mill, Franklin County, Virginia, that Mary (Williams?) Wright died between 1805 and 1808 at Boone Mill, Franklin County, Virginia, and that William Wright and Mary (Williams?) Wright had the following child:

1)   James Wright, born in 1756 or 1757 at Fauquier County, Virginia.
The source reference on which this conclusion was based was not given.

<u>Genealogy Of John J. Wright Of Virginia, Indiana and Kansas</u> by John Calvin Wright, 5624 Western Avenue, Chevy Chase, Maryland, 1953, stated that Charles Arthur Hoppin in <u>Tyler's Quarterly</u> had identified the William Wright whose will was probated in 1806 at Fauquier County as the son of John Wright and Elizabeth (Darnell) Wright, but asserted that this identification was mistaken:

> page 42: "[Mr. Hoppin] . . . . cautioned his readers against confusing the two William Wrights of Fauquier County with each other.
>
> Much caution is needed to keep them separate. However the author finds that Mr. Hoppin failed to observe his advice to others and jumped to a hasty conclusion in closing his treatment of William[5] the eldest son of John[4] and brother to John[5] of whom Mr. Hoppin had occasion to write at much greater length since he had been employed to write up the genealogical ancestry of certain descendants of John[5] but not of descendants of William[5].
>
> On page 182 of Vol. 1, Nos. 3, Jan. 1920, of Tyler's Quarterly Mr. Hoppin summarizes concerning the children of John[4]. In Item (6) he assumes that a Will proved at Warrenton, April 28, 1806 and signed by a William Wright is the Will of William[5], son of John[4] Wright, Gentleman, of whom he treated. This hasty assumption is in error for the following reasons:"

Mr. Wright then identified some of the documents referred to above which indicate that 1809 William Wright of Franklin County resided in Fauquier County prior to residing in Franklin County, including the Fauquier County deeds naming William and Mary Wright and the Fauquier County lawsuit for debt against William Wright and the summons in that case that indicated he did not reside in Fauquier County in 1763 and the signature comparison of the promissory note signed by William Wright in Fauquier County that was the subject of that lawsuit and the signature of William Wright on his will in Franklin County.

> But Mr. Wright also stated that William Wright married Mary Williams:
>
> page 26: "William[5] son of John[4] and Elizabeth (Darnall) Wright was born in 1727-8 at "Leesylvania" near Dumfries, Va. He married Mary Williams in 1746-7 and died at Boone Mill, Franklin Co., Va. in 1808. He was buried in Franklin Co. near the town of Boone Mill. Mary was born in Virginia about 1727-8 and died shortly before her husband. She also was buried near Boone Mill. After their marriage William and Mary settled in Fauquier County "on the south side of Pig Nut Ridge" and engaged in the business of farming. The marriage records for Fauquier County have been lost so far as our William[5], and his elder sons John[6] and

William[6] Jr. are concerned. William[5] left Fauquier County between 1762 and 1771. Hence John[6] and William[6] may have been married in Fauquier County or in what was then a part of Bedford (now Franklin) County Va. Here again we have no records of marriages until 1786. . . ."

It is unclear on what John Calvin Wright based his identification of Mary Williams as the wife of 1809 William Wright and no documentation was given for that identification.

International Genealogical Index, Batch 773110657 and 773110656, Film 1126151, and by Lois Diane Smith stated that William Wright was a son of John Wright and Elizabeth (Darnall) Wright, was born in 1727 at Dumfries, Virginia, married Mary Williams, and died in 1808, and that William Wright and Mary (Williams) Wright had the following child:

1)   James Wright, born in 1736 at Fauquier County, Virginia.

The source record for this information was stated to be a printed family record compiled by John Wright, presumably Genealogy Of John J. Wright Of Virginia, Indiana and Kansas by John Calvin Wright and, therefore, provides no further support for the conclusion that William Wright, the son of 1792 John Wright, married a Mary Williams.

Each of these identifications of William Wright as married to a Mary Williams was probably based on Fauquier County Deeds 1/433 and 1/435 in which William and Mary Wright and David and Betty Williams joined together to sell land in Fauquier County. This looks like a deed by heirs who have inherited the land and thus would indicate that Mary Wright was a Mary (Williams) Wright joining with her brother David in the sale of the land. As set forth above, Roger Morris has made clear that David Williams' joinder in the deed was merely to remove any cloud on title in the hands of the purchaser because of the irregular sale of the land by his mother Ann (Darnall) (Williams) Garner to 1792 John Wright of Fauquier County and, therefore, Mary Wright was not Mary (Williams) Wright. In addition, as set forth above, the will of David Williams' father Jonas Williams did not list a daughter Mary. There is, therefore, no supported documentation that Mary, the wife of William Wright, was Mary (Williams) Wright.

Second Alternative: William Wright Who Married Elizabeth Thompson

The second alternative identification is that the William Wright who married Elizabeth Thompson was the son of 1792 John Wright of Fauquier County.

In <u>Records Of Wright and Kindred Families</u> by Lottie Wright Davis, 1966, she identified William Wright, the son of 1792 John Wright of Fauquier County, as married to Elizabeth Thompson:

> "William Wright I, Gentleman, Vestryman and Lieut., son of Judge John Wright and Elizabeth (Darnall) Wright, b. Nov. 1740 at "Sylvania," Prince William Co., Va., d. April 25, 1806 in Leeds Parish Fauquier Co., Va., m. Dec. 25, 1768 Elizabeth Thompson of Albemarle Co., Va., b. Nov. 7, 1750, d. July 8, 1810. Issue:
>
> 1. William Wright, Jr., b. Dec. 7, 1769, d. Aug 27, 1834.
> 2. Joseph Thompson Wright, b. about 1772.
> 3. Sarah Woodson Wright, b. about 1775, m. about 1795, Mr. _____ Evans.
> 4. Edward Wright, b. about 1778.
> 5. Mary Wright, b. about 1781, m. 1799 Joshua LaMart.
>
> After William Wright I returned home from the War of the Revolution, he and his family continued to live near his father's estate "Pine View" in the southern part of Fauquier Co., Va. Tax records disclose for the year 1783 their taxes listed together (which included taxes on 32 horses) Records disclose that William Wright sold his land in 1785 and moved his family in 1786 to property he had purchased in the northern part of Fauquier County in what is still known as Leeds Parish - where he spent the remainder of his life of twenty years. Lieut. William Wright's will is recorded in Will Book 4, page 205, Warrenton, Fauquier Co., Virginia. It is dated August 20, 1805, approved Aprl 29, 1806. . . .
> [quote of will omitted here] . . . . He appointed his eldest son William, Jr. as executor - witnesses were his wife, sons Joseph and Edward, and the will was approved by daughters Sarah Wright Evans and Mary Wright LaMart.
>
> The wife, Elizabeth Thompson Wright, died July 8, 1810. An appraisement of the estate was recorded July 23, 1810, and also administrator's account."

It is clear from this account that Ms. Davis is continuing the identification of 1805 William Wright of Fauquier County as the son of 1792 John Wright of Fauquier County and for the reasons set forth above, that is incorrect.

Interestingly, although Ms. Davis appears to be acquainted with some of the information from the family record of 1834 William Wright, the son of 1805 William Wright of Fauquier County, she apparently did not see the actual family record which clearly listed Elizabeth Lloyd, not Elizabeth Thompson, as the wife of 1805 William Wright of Fauquier County and stated that Elizabeth (Lloyd) Wright died on July 25, 1830, not July 8, 1810. There is no indication regarding what Ms. Davis relied on to identify Elizabeth Thompson as the wife of 1805 William Wright or her death on July 8, 1810.

It is also unclear on what Ms. Davis relied to assert that William Wright sold his land in southern Fauquier County in 1785 and moved to northern Fauquier County in 1786. As set forth above, 1805 William Wright first purchased land in Fauquier County on September 5, 1780, and sold that land on April 7, 1794. The only other William Wright deed in that time period was by 1789 William Wright of Spotsylvania County dated on April 24, 1789. There were no deeds recorded by a William Wright in Fauquier County in 1785 or 1786.

The identification of William Wright who married Elizabeth Thompson as the son of 1792 John Wright of Fauquier County remains an unsupported assertion that is inconsistent with the known evidence.

Summary Of Alternative Identifications

The result is that these two alternative identifications of William Wright, the son of 1792 John Wright of Fauquier County, are either incorrect or unsupported by evidence.

Part Eleven: Summary Of Information About 1809 William Wright Of Franklin County And Mary (Grant) Wright In Northern Virginia

The evidence set forth above presents a strong case for the identification of 1809 William Wright of Franklin County as probably the son of 1792 John Wright of Fauquier County. With that identification, it is appropriate to summarize in chronological order the records and what is known regarding 1809 William Wright and his wife Mary (Grant) Wright in northern Virginia, including some additional documents that were not necessary to the arguments set forth above.

60

The will of Elizabeth (Bronaugh) (Darnell) Wright's first husband Waugh Darnall was probated on October 7, 1726, and the will of her father Jeremiah Bronaugh dated on April 14, 1736, listed her as Elizabeth Wright. This indicates that 1792 John Wright and Elizabeth (Bronaugh) (Darnell) Wright were married between October 7, 1726, and April 14, 1736. The marriage was probably after 1726 and thus perhaps in 1727, and if that were correct, then their first child would have been born probably in 1728. Also as set forth above, William Wright and Mary (Grant) Wright were married before September 4, 1751, and their son John Wright was born in about 1749 or possibly 1747, indicating that they were married in 1748 or possibly 1746. Such a marriage date indicates that William Wright was probably born in about 1728 or 1729. The convergence of these records suggests that William Wright, the son of 1792 John Wright of Fauquier County, was probably born in about 1728 or possibly 1729.

The Washington Ancestry by Charles Arthur Hoppin identified 1792 John Wright's father as 1729/30 John Wright of Stafford County and stated that 1729/30 John Wright moved in 1723 from Cople Parish, Westmoreland County, to land purchased from Henry Lee on Powell's Run in a part of Stafford County which became Prince William County.

Prince William County, Virginia, was formed on March 25, 1731, from King George and Stafford Counties. The Washington Ancestry by Charles Arthur Hoppin stated that 1792 John Wright of Fauquier County was appointed on April 27, 1731, as one of the first justices of Prince William County.

1729/30 John Wright, the probable father of 1792 John Wright, resided in a part of Stafford County that became Prince William County from 1723 until his death in 1729/30 and 1792 John Wright was made a justice of Prince William County upon its formation in 1731 and, therefore would have been residing there at the time of his appointment and probably during the period his father resided there as well. If 1809 William Wright was born in 1728 or possibly 1729, then he would have been born before the formation of Prince William County and, therefore, probably at his father's residence in Stafford County in the part that became Prince William County in 1731.

The will of William Grant, Jr., undated and probated on May 4, 1733, at King George County, Virginia, W.B. A-1/98 listed Mary Grant as one of his daughters, indicating that she was born before May 4, 1733.

The will of William Grant, Sr., dated January 24, 1726/7 and a nuncupative codicil dated January 4, 1733/4 and probated on February 1, 1733/4, at King George County, Virginia, W.B. A-1/101 made a gift to his son William Grant's children,

On February 3, 1743, at King George County, Virginia, Fiduciary Account Book 3/18 John Grant filed his accounting for his guardianship of Mary Grant and her sister Elizabeth Grant for the period from May 6, 1738, to at least 1741, indicating that both daughters were born after about 1723.

On August 25, 1751, at Prince William County D.B. M/169 1792 John Wright of Fauquier County gifted 185 acres of land to his son William Wright and the deed contained a notation that it was delivered to William Wright in 1762. This record indicates that William Wright was old enough to be living on his own land in Hamilton Parish, Prince William County, in 1751 and, therefore, is evidence that he was born probably before 1733.

On September 4, 1751, at King George County, Virginia, D.B. 1743-1752/442 William Wright and Mary his wife sold to Jane Payne one moiety of 180 acres of land inherited by Mary (Grant) Wright from her father William Grant, the younger. If Mary (Grant) Wright was at least 18 years of age when she married, then she was probably born before about September 1733.

On September 24, 1759, at Fauquier County, Virginia, D.B. 1/65 William Wright and Timothy Stamps were both witnesses to a deed from James Scott to Thomas Stamps.

The Washington Ancestry by Charles Arthur Hoppin stated that on September 27, 1759, at Fauquier County, Virginia, Court Minute Book 1/25 William Wright's military service was of record when "John Wright Present . . . John Cole, Elias Edmonds, William Wright, Armistead Churchill etc. Captains, took the usual oaths to his Majesty's person and Government and subscribed the Test."

In 1759 Captain William Wright incurred an account debt for 6£ 16s for 18 barrels of Indian corn, a copy of which account was filed in the case of Chadwell v. Wright, Fauquier County, Virginia, Chancery Court Loose Papers, Ended Causes 1763, Box 7:

"1759 Capt. William Wright   Dr £ S d
To 18 Barrells of Indian Corn @ 10/
   9 0 0
Cr By Cash paid

  2 4 0

  £6 16 0
. . . ."

On February 8, 1760, William Wright executed a promissory note payable to John Chadwell for the account due of 6£ 16s, a copy of which note was filed in the case of Chadwell v. Wright, Fauquier County, Virginia, Chancery Court Loose Papers, Ended Causes 1763, Box 7.

On February 28, 1761, at Fauquier County, Virginia, Chancery Court Loose Papers, Box 3/1761-003, William Wright, Jr., executed a surety bond for 51£ 6S 2p to secure Peter Hon.

On about November 27, 1761, in Triplett v. Wright, Fauquier County, Virginia, Chancery Court Loose Papers, Ended Causes 1763-9-112, William Wright executed his surety bond for the payment of 18£ 5s 9p due to Francis Triplett.

On November 27, 1761, in Triplett v. Wright, Fauquier County, Virginia, Chancery Court Loose Papers, Ended Causes 1763-9-112, a summons was issued against William Wright to answer the complaint of Francis Triplett for the payment of 36£ 11s 6p due on William Wright's surety bond, with the indication that he was not found, but a copy was left, presumably at his residence.

On about February 27, 1762, in How v. Wright, Fauquier County, Virginia, Chancery Court Loose Papers, Box 3/1761-003, Peter How filed a complaint for payment of 51£ 6s 2p due from William Wright on his bond dated February 28, 1761.

On February 27, 1762, in How v. Wright, Fauquier County, Virginia, Chancery Court Loose Papers, Box 3/1761-003, a summons was issued against William Wright, Jr., to answer the complaint of Peter How for payment of 51£ 6s 2p. The use of the term "Jr." in the summons was to distinguish this William Wright from 1789 William Wright of Fredericksburg, who was older than this William Wright and, therefore, identifies the William Wright of this suit as 1809 William Wright of Franklin County, the son of 1792 John Wright of Fauquier County. The resolution of the case of How v. Wright has not as yet been found.

On June 25, 1762, in Mercer v. Wright, Fauquier County, Virginia, Chancery Court Loose Papers, Ended Causes Box 8, Folder 7, William Wright of Fauquier County executed a promissory note payable to James Mercer for 4£ 2s 6p.

On August 26, 1762, at Fauquier County, Virginia, D.B. 1/369 William Wright and Mary Wright sold to Thomas Edwards 125 acres of the land gifted to William sold by his father John Wright.

On October 14, 1762, at Fauquier County, Virginia, D.B. 1/433 William Wright and Mary Wright and David Williams and Betty Williams sold to John Waddle for 60 acres of the land gifted to William Wright by his father John Wright.

On March 25, 1763, in Triplett v. Wright, Fauquier County, Virginia, Chancery Court Loose Papers, Ended Causes 1763-9-112, an attachment was issued against William Wright for payment of the debt due to Francis Triplett and on the defendant's failure to appear, the sheriff attached one candle mold.

On about March 28, 1763, in Chadwell v. Wright, Fauquier County, Virginia, Chancery Court Loose Papers, Ended Causes 1763, Box 7, John Chadwell filed suit for payment of the promissory note due to him.

On March 28, 1763, in Chadwell v. Wright, Fauquier County, Virginia, Chancery Court Loose Papers, Ended Causes 1763, Box 7, a summons was issued against William Wright to answer John Chadwell in his suit for payment of the promissory note due to him and the summons was returned with the notation that William Wright was not found, but a copy was left, presumably at his residence.

On May 28, 1763, in Chadwell v. Wright, Fauquier County, Virginia, Chancery Court Loose Papers, Ended Causes 1763, Box 7, a second summons was issued against William Wright to answer John Chadwell in his suit for payment of the promissory note due to him and the summons was returned with the notation that the summons had been executed on William Wright and his body was in gaol.

On June 13, 1763, John Chadwell assigned the account due to him from Captain William Wright to Richard Bryan, a copy of which assignment was filed in the case of Chadwell v. Wright, Fauquier County, Virginia, Chancery Court Loose Papers, Ended Causes 1763, Box 7.

Sometime in approximately 1763 and probably after May 28 a jury in Chadwell v. Wright, Fauquier County, Virginia, Chancery Court Loose Papers, Ended Causes 1763, Box 7, found for the plaintiff.

On about August 1, 1763, in Mercer v. Wright, Fauquier County, Virginia, Chancery Court Loose Papers, Ended Causes Box 8, Folder 7, James Mercer filed a complaint against William Wright for payment of the promissory note of 4£ 2s 6p due to him.

On August 1, 1763, in Mercer v. Wright, Fauquier County, Virginia, Chancery Court Loose Papers, Ended Causes Box 8, Folder 7, a summons was issued against William Wright to answer the complaint of James Mercer for payment of the promissory note of 4£ 2s 6p.

Genealogy Of John J. Wright Of Virginia, Indiana and Kansas by John Calvin Wright stated that on August 29, 1763, William Wright executed a promissory note for six pounds one shilling and by January 28, 1764, was not to be found in Fauquier County.

On June 1, 1785, John Wright named William Wright as a son in his will probated on February 27, 1792, at Fauquier County, Virginia, W.B. 2/219, and referred to William as having been given land by John Wright which William Wright had sold.

By 1768 William Wright and his wife Mary (Grant) Wright were in Bedford County, Virginia, in a part which became Franklin County, Virginia, and lived there for the remainder of their lives.

INDEX

Darnell, Elizabeth, 16
Darnell, Elizabeth (____), 14
Darnell, Waugh, 13, 14, 16
Davis, Lottie Wright, 59
Dean, Charles, 27
Dean, John Thomas, 40
Deane, Charles, 27
Dickinson, Doris G, 43
Doniphan, Anderson, 15, 28
Dudley, Dorothy, 9
Durham, Dorothy, 9
Edmonds, Elias, 35, 62
Edmonds Jr, Wm, 16
Edwards, Thomas, 23, 35, 64, 41
Ellis, Mary, 30, 34
Etteridge, Francis, 26
Evans, John, 34
Evans, Sarah Wright, 59
Fairfax, Thomas Lord, 31
Fallon, P. D, 52
Forbes, Otey, 52
Fossaker, Capt. Richard, 34
Fossaker, Richard, 30
Frazier, John, 37
Frazier, Martha, 37
Garner, Ann (Darnall) (Williams), 18, 22,
   24, 25, 58
Garner, Anne, 18, 19
Garner, Charles, 18, 19, 22, 24, 25
Garner, Vincent, 22
Garner, William, 30
Garnett, James, 10
Gatewood, Dorothy, 9
Gearhart, John, 52, 53
Gilbert, Elisha K, 52
Gouldman, Dorothy, 9
Grant, Captain John, 30
Grant, Daniel, 26
Grant, Eliza, 27
Grant, Elizabeth, 28, 38, 62
Grant, Elizabeth (____), 50
Grant, John, 26, 27, 28, 49, 50, 62
Grant, Margaret (Bronaugh), 50
Grant, Mary, 27, 28, 29, 38, 62
Grant, Rosamond, 30

Grant, William, 26, 27, 28, 38, 62
Grant, William M, 26
Grant, Willim, 26
Grant, Jr, William, 27, 28, 49, 62
Grant Junr, William, 27
Grant, Sr., William, 26, 50, 62
Grayson, Benjamin, 6
Greer, Captain Moses, 51
Greer, John, 41
Gresham, Benjamin, 7
Grubbs, Thomas, 24
Hackney, Willm, 5
Hall, John, 41
Hanton, Hon Eppa, 52
Harrison, Burr, 5
Harrison, George, 29
Harrison, Thomas, 5
Harrison, Wm, 5
Henry, Dorothy, 9
Hon, Peter, 44, 63
Hoppin, Charles, 3, 5, 6, 7, 8, 9, 12, 13,
   17
Hoppin, Charles Arthur, 2, 3, 9, 12, 17,
   34, 38, 57, 61, 62
Houston, Thomas, 55
How, Peter, 64
Hudnal, John, 32, 33
Hudnal, Joseph, 5
Hudnall, John, 32, 33
Huston, Sarah, 55
Huston, Tabitha (Wright), 55
Huston, Thomas, 55
Jones, Robert, 5
Judd, Isaac, 23
Kay, Elizabeth, 34
Keith, Thomas, 21
Kerns, William, 21
King, Sanford, 29
LaMart, Joshua, 59
LaMart, Mary Wright, 59
Lee, Henry, 3, 4, 6, 7, 17, 61
Lemert, Joshua, 34
Linton, Willm, 5
Lloyd, Elizabeth, 36, 39, 60
Lloyd, John, 22

Wright, Catherine (Doran), 55
Wright, Constant, 29
Wright, Dorothy, 9
Wright, Dorothy (____), 3, 4, 10
Wright, Dr. Luke F, 12
Wright, Edward, 59
Wright, Elizabeth, 15, 16, 20, 36, 37, 40,
    61
Wright, Elizabeth (____), 21
Wright, Elizabeth (Abshire), 55
Wright, Elizabeth (Bronaugh) (Darnall),
    1, 13, 15, 16, 49, 50, 61
Wright, Elizabeth (Darnall?), 56
Wright, Elizabeth (Darnall), 36, 57, 58,
    59
Wright, Elizabeth (Darnell), 57
Wright, Elizabeth (Lloyd), 36, 38, 60
Wright, Enoch, 54, 55, 56
Wright, Ezekeil, 53
Wright, Ezekiel, 52, 53
Wright, Francis, 4, 6, 7, 8, 13, 17
Wright, Francis, 18
Wright, George, 49, 53, 54
Wright, J. C, 52
Wright, James, 15, 16, 20, 21, 35, 49,
53, 54, 56, 58
Wright, James Grant, 49
Wright, John, 1, 2, 3, 4, 5, 6, 7, 8, 9, 10,
    11, 12, 13, 15, 16, 17, 18, 19, 20, 21,
    22, 23, 24, 25, 26, 29, 30, 31, 32, 33,
    34, 35, 36, 37, 38, 39, 41, 42, 43, 44
    49, 50, 51, 52, 53, 54, 55, 56, 57, 58,
    59, 60, 61, 62, 64, 65
Wright, John A, 55
Wright, John Calvin, 43, 44, 52, 57, 58,
    65
Wright, John J, 43, 52, 57, 65
Wright, Joseph, 53, 59
Wright, Joseph Thompson, 59
Wright, Maj. Francis, 2, 3, 36
Wright, Major James, 15
Wright, Majr Francis, 4
Wright, Mary, 20, 21, 23, 24, 25, 28, 30,
    31, 38, 41, 42, 50, 57, 58, 59, 62, 64

Wright, Mary (____), 21, 25, 36, 42, 49,
    53, 55
Wright, Mary (Brent), 29, 31, 32
Wright, Mary (Grant), 1, 2, 26, 29, 31,
    38, 49, 50, 53, 60, 61, 62, 65
Wright, Mary (Williams?), 56
Wright, Mary (Williams), 58
Wright, Mary (Wray), 55
Wright, Matthew, 55
Wright, Matthew W, 55, 56
Wright, Richard, 2, 4, 13, 30, 34
Wright, Richd, 34
Wright, Rosamond, 20, 21, 29, 30, 32,
    33
Wright, Rosamond [Rosanna], 30
Wright, Rosanna, 30
Wright, Rose, 29
Wright, Sarah (Huston), 55, 56
Wright, Sarah Woodson, 59
Wright, Sarah [Huston], 55
Wright, Thomas, 53
Wright, William, 1, 2, 19, 20, 21, 22, 23,
    24, 25, 26, 28, 29, 30, 31, 32, 33, 34,
    35, 36, 37, 38, 39, 40, 41, 42, 43, 44,
    45, 49, 50, 53, 54, 55, 56, 57, 58, 59,
    60, 61, 62, 63, 64, 65
Wright, Winfield, 29
Wright, Wingfield, 49
Wright, Winkfield, 55
Wright, Wm, 38
Wright, Dorothy (____), 3
Wright, William, 3
Wright, William Grant, 49
Wright, Dorothy (Awbrey), 9, 12
Wright, James, 21
Wright, Jr, James Grant, 49
Wright, Jr, William, 35, 59, 63, 64
Wright Junr, William, 44
Wright, Senior, John, 5
Wright Senr, William, 43
Wright, Sr., John, 52, 53
Wright, Sr., William, 35

Heritage Books by Robert N. Grant

Lynchburg

Wright Family Records: Lynchburg, Virginia Birth Records (1853–1896), Marriage Records (1805–1900), Marriage Notices (1794–1880), Census Records (1900), Deed Records (1805–1900), Death Records (1853–1896), Probate Records (1805–1900)

Amherst County

Wright Family Birth Records, 1853–1896; Marriage Records, 1761–1900; Census Records, 1810–1900, in Amherst County, Virginia

Wright Family Land Tax Records: Amherst County, Virginia, 1782–1850

Wright Family Patent Deeds and Land Grants, 1761–1900, Deed Records, 1761–1903; Chancery Court Files, 1804–1900; Death Records, 1853–1920; Cemetery Records by Cemetery; and Probate Records, 1761–1900, in Amherst County, Virginia

Wright Family Personal Property Tax Lists: Amherst County, Virginia, 1782–1850

Appomattox County

Wright Family Birth Records, Marriage Records, and Personal Property Tax Lists: Appomattox County, Virginia

Wright Family Census Records, Deed Records, Land Tax Lists, Death Records and Probate Records: Appomattox County, Virginia

Bedford County

Wright Family Census Records: Bedford County, Virginia, 1810–1900

Wright Family Death, Cemetery and Probate Records: Bedford County, Virginia

Wright Family Land Records: Bedford County, Virginia

Wright Family Personal Property Tax Records for Bedford County, Virginia, 1782 to 1850

Wright Family Records: Births in Bedford County, Virginia

Wright Family Records: Land Tax List, Bedford County, Virginia, 1782–1850

Wright Family Records: Marriages in Bedford County, Virginia

Campbell County

Wright Family Birth Records (1853–1896) and Marriage Records (1782–1900): Campbell County, Virginia

Wright Family Census Records: Campbell County, Virginia, 1810–1900

Wright Family Death Records (1853–1920), Cemetery Records by Cemetery, and Probate Records (1782–1900): Campbell County, Virginia

Wright Family Deed Records (1782–1900) and Land Tax List (1782–1850): Campbell County, Virginia

Wright Family Personal Property Tax Lists: Campbell County, Virginia, 1785–1850

Cumberland County

Wright Family Birth, Marriage, Personal Property Tax and Census Records, Cumberland County, Virginia

Wright Family Deed, Land Tax, Death and Probate Records, Cumberland County, Virginia

Essex County

Wright Family Birth, Marriage, and Personal Property Tax Records, Essex County, Virginia

Wright Family Census, Deed, Land Tax, Death and Probate Records, Essex County, Virginia

Fauquier County

The Identification of 1792 John Wright of Fauquier County, Virginia, as Not the Son of 1792/30 John Wright of Stafford County, Virginia

Franklin County

The Identification of 1809 William Wright of Franklin County, Virginia, as the Son of 1792 John Wright of Fauquier County, Virginia, and Elizabeth (Bronaugh) (Darnall) Wright

Wright Family Birth Records (1853–1896) and Marriage Records (1788–1915): Franklin County, Virginia, 1853–1896

Wright Family Census Records: Franklin County, Virginia, 1810–1900

Wright Family Death Records (1854–1920), Cemetery Records by Cemetery, and Probate Records (1785–1928): Franklin County, Virginia

Wright Family Land Grants (1785–1900) and Deed Records (1785–1897): Franklin County, Virginia

Wright Family Land Tax Lists: Franklin County, Virginia, 1786–1860

Wright Family Personal Property Tax Lists: Franklin County, Virginia, 1786–1850

Goochland County

Identifying the Wrights in the Goochland County, Virginia Tithe Lists, 1732–84

Montgomery County

Wright Family Birth, Marriage, and Personal Property Tax Records, Montgomery County, Virginia

Wright Family Census, Land Grants, Land Tax, Deed, Death, and Probate Records, Montgomery County, Virginia

Nelson County

Wright Family Birth Records, 1853–1896; Marriage Records, 1808–1910; Census Records, 1810–1900; Patent Deeds and Land Grants; Deed Records, 1808–1910; Death Records, 1853–1896; Probate Records, 1808–1900, in Nelson County, Virginia

Wright Family Land Tax Records: Nelson County, Virginia, 1809–1850

Wright Family Personal Property Tax Lists: Nelson County, Virginia, 1809–1850

Prince Edward County

Wright Family Land Grants, Deed Records, Land Tax List, Death Records, Probate Records: Prince Edward County, Virginia

Wright Family Records: Prince Edward County, Virginia Birth Records, Marriage Records, Election Polls, and Tithe List, Personal Property Tax List, Census

Rockbridge County

Wright Family Birth Records, 1853–1896; Marriage Records, 1777–1918; Census Records, 1810–1900; Deed Records, 1777–1902; Death Records, 1853–1896; Cemetery Records, and Probate Records, 1777–1909; in Rockbridge County, Virginia

Wright Family Land Tax Lists: Rockbridge County, Virginia, 1782–1850

Wright Family Personal Property Tax Lists: Rockbridge County, Virginia, 1782–1850

www.ingramcontent.com/pod-product-compliance
Lightning Source LLC
Chambersburg PA
CBHW081421270326
41931CB00015B/3363